I0459310

THE POWER WITHIN
Finding Strength, Voice & Vision

A collection of true stories
from women who rose, rebuilt, and remembered who they are.

Presented by the Women's Empower Network
Published by Printed Matters Publishing LLC

With contributions by:
Sol Alé Jini, Founder & Creator
Amy Brotherson • Beth Golden • Ann-Marie Lorde
Diana Concoff Morgan • Hadassah Rose • Inthirani Arul
Kate Kaplan • Katherine T. Moyer • Nicolette Halladay
Peggy Sue Conner • Pia Becker • Suelynn Silva • Terri Tonkin

With Gratitude, proceeds from this year's book sales (minus fees) will be donated to these organizations making a difference in our community.

is a change-maker for survivors of domestic and sexual violence.

Supporting Community in Nutrition, Health & Belonging

Cultivate an Environment of Success for Adults with Developmental Disabilities

CONTENTS

INTRODUCTION
THE POWER WITHIN

*W*hen you open this book, you're not just reading it, you're stepping into a circle rich with experiences. Not a polished sanctuary, but a real space designed by scars, stories, and realities. The women here have walked through fire, silence, heartbreak, and reinvention, but the beauty about this is that they did not return empty-handed. They came back with treasures of wisdom, with courage, and with a record of what it takes to bounce back when life seems to knock you down.

This collection is not a glossy triumph. It is the unfiltered choreography of breaking and becoming, of losing your footing and learning to stand again. If you've carried doubt, fatigue, or the echo of a relentless voice saying "not enough," you will find yourself here. And you will also recognize that even in the darkest seasons, there's a power within us that endures, waiting patiently to be remembered.

Strength

Strength is never the absence of struggle; but the willingness to face your struggles head-on. In this book,

Kate shows us the raw courage it takes to survive the relentless demands of caregiving, carrying love and exhaustion in equal measure. Her story honors every sleepless night and every unseen act of devotion, reminding us that sometimes strength looks like simply showing up when you'd rather collapse.

Amy traces resilience through seasons of change, refusing to let transitions define her as broken. She shows that true strength emerges when we let life redirect us, shaping a deeper core rather than eroding it.

Hadassah shares her journey of standing steady in life's storms that threatened to consume her. She reminds us that faith, lived daily and practiced in the grit of reality, is not soft comfort but a solid foundation that keeps us upright.

Inthirani demonstrates that compassion is not weakness but power —especially when directed toward ourselves. Her story reminds us that strength grows when we treat our own wounds with the same care we've always offered others.

Nicolette transforms the pain of loss into a foundation for growth. Through her, we see that strength is not in avoiding heartbreak but in allowing it to deepen our humanity and sharpen our purpose.

Katherine embodies strength in the decision to leave the familiar behind and step into the unknown. Her courage to walk a new path proves that strength is not about clinging—it is about releasing what no longer fits and trusting the next step.

Here, strength isn't a highlight reel. It's late nights, hard choices, and the quiet decision to stand again, even when no one is watching.

Transition: Strength → Voice

Strength alone isn't enough. It steadies us, but without expression, it remains hidden, waiting. What transforms strength into connection is our voice—the moment we dare to name what we've carried, speak the truths we've kept tucked away, and allow others to hear them.

Voice

If strength steadies us, voice carries us forward.

Terri shows how advocacy becomes courage in motion. Her willingness to stand up and speak out reminds us that voice isn't just for ourselves—it's often the lifeline to someone else who desperately needs to hear those words from your voice.

Pia demonstrates the grit of persistence, finding her voice by refusing to let setbacks silence her. Her story reveals that voice is built, choice by choice, in every moment we refuse to shrink back.

Peggy Sue writes her truth after years of carrying it quietly, discovering freedom in the act. Now, she teaches us that voice isn't about crafting the perfect story but about daring to speak the real one.

Diana shows that voice can also emerge through quiet leadership. You don't need to shout to be heard; sometimes it's the steady, consistent presence and actions that changes a room, and even a life the most.

Jini reclaims the voice she once set aside, proving that it's never too late to say yes again. Her story reminds us that silence isn't the end —our voice waits for us, and the moment we choose to use it, everything begins to take form.

Together, these women show us that voice doesn't require permission. It demands honesty. And every time one woman claims hers, she opens space for others to rise.

Transition: Voice → Vision

When strength meets voice, something deeper and larger begins to stir. The moment you realize you can stand and dare to speak, that moment vision comes alive. Vision becomes the clarity that shows us more than survival, guiding us toward the possibilities of life.

Vision

Vision is the thread that pulls us forward, toward what's next.

Ann Marie shows us what happens when you name what you're building and take the steps to move toward achieving it. Her story reminds us that vision starts with clarity—and clarity has the power to change a life.

Beth teaches that vision often emerges from the choice to face the future with courage. Even when our current state or path seems uncertain, it becomes the compass that directs our steps.

Katherine, who already showed us what strength looks like in leaving the familiar behind, proves that vision is born in that very act. The moment she chose differently, she began writing a new future.

Jini, whose reclaimed voice marked a turning point, demonstrates how vision returns the moment we dare to say yes again. She says, dreams never truly vanish, they only wait patiently for our agreement.

Suelynn brings vision to life through awakening, daring to dream, and believing in what once seemed impossible. From declaring, "This is not my life," to creating homes, adventures, and healing practices that once felt out of reach, her journey proves that vision is not wishful thinking, it is a blueprint for transformation. Even in grief, she carries her vision forward, turning loss into purpose and lighting the path for others to follow.

Vision is not fragile, it is faithful. It waits for us to stop hiding, to step forward without the full picture, and to trust that possibility is still alive. The women in these chapters show us that vision grows stronger each time we dare to believe in it.

An Invitation

This book is written to serve as both a mirror and a map. In these pages, you will see yourself reflected—in resilience, in self-doubt, in courage, and in the choice to keep going. You will also find direction and gentle reminders that your strength is still here, your voice still matters, and your vision is still alive.

The Power Within is not just a concept. It is a reality within you. These stories are gathered to remind you that your past does not disqualify or define you, that silence does not define you, and that waiting does not diminish you. They will show you that the same strength, voice, and vision alive in these women is also alive in you.

So here is the invitation: Don't just read these pages—enter them. Let the experiences shared within—inspire you. Let them comfort you. Let them provoke you and move you toward your possibilities. Let them remind you that your scars are not the end of your story; they are proof of your survival and seeds of your strength. Let them stir your voice and sharpen your vision.

As you read, remember this: you are not broken, even if it may feel that way. That feeling is part of the process—a journey of awakening into something new and beautiful. And the power you've been waiting for has been inside you all along.

Because the power within you is real. It is time to step into remembering that which has always been there.

1

THE OTHER SIDE OF BURNT TOAST

BY SOL ALÉ JINI

*T*he Daredevil and the Candy Hustle

Long before anyone handed me a microphone, invited me to speak, or called me a leader, I was already leading. Not in boardrooms or on stages, but from my neighborhood and sandy streets of Miami Beach, barefoot and brazen, with scraped knees and a wild glint in my eye.

I was nine years old, and freedom was the only currency I understood. Back then, I didn't follow, I led. Not because anyone told me I should, but because something deep inside me refused to sit still.

It was the early '60s, and our playground was the whole neighborhood. My younger brother and I were inseparable co-conspirators, full of curiosity and with zero regard for what was considered "appropriate." Our biggest thrill was trekking to the 1st Street Pier with a gang of local kids, daring each other to jump off and timing our dives with the waves—trusting the sea to rise fast enough to cushion the dive. Three feet of water felt like the deep end to us. It was reckless, sure. But we weren't afraid. We were alive.

When we weren't flying off piers, we were scaling coconut trees and scavenging coconuts. We weren't allowed to touch machetes, so we'd pry the husks open with a claw hammer and a screwdriver—probably more dangerous, definitely more creative. Once cracked, we'd load the coconuts into our little red wagon and haul them to the corner grocery store. There, we'd station ourselves out front, selling them for ten cents apiece.

We weren't trying to save money. We were trying to buy sugar. With our thirty cents, we'd march into what felt like a candy palace and come out with pockets full of sweet loot. It was never about profit; it was about possibility. We had an idea, we acted on it, and that rush —the thrill of turning nothing into something—stayed with me far longer than the candy ever did.

Looking back now, I see more than just a mischievous kid with a spark of boldness and entrepreneurial flair. I see someone already stepping into leadership and practicing its essence even without knowing it. Vision. Initiative. Courage. Follow-through. I didn't know what "entrepreneur" meant. I didn't understand the language of strategy or momentum. I didn't know what it meant to mobilize a team or spark enthusiasm. All I knew was that I could make something happen. So I did.

That spirit carried me into adolescence and beyond. I never hesitated to step up. As a young adult, I organized company picnics without a second thought. I gladly rallied coworkers to pitch in, build something fun, and create a sense of community in the workplace. Leadership, in those moments, felt natural, almost effortless. But when the stakes got higher and the spotlight grew brighter, something inside me quietly pulled back.

When a real opportunity knocked, I hesitated.

Years later, I was offered the chance to run my own department at a major oil company. It was a big step up, a moment many would've called a dream come true. But I was two months pregnant with my second child, and the commute alone would've taken three hours out of each day. As much as I was honored, I turned it down.

Instead, I chose early retirement and packed up my life. I left my husband and with my 3 1/2-month-old and 4-year-old and moved to Albuquerque—a city where I didn't know a single soul. Once again, I began anew. This time, as a single mother, a woman in transition… and an entrepreneur on the edge of becoming.

The 14-Year-Old and the Soul Whisper

I was fourteen when the ground fell out from beneath me.

There's no poetic way to say it: I was violated by someone I knew. What followed was an abortion I didn't choose, a wave of disbelief I didn't understand, and silence from the adults who should have fought for me. The pain wasn't just in what happened—it was in how it was handled. No justice. No comfort. No acknowledgment. Just a silent, aching void where protection should have lived.

But in that darkness, something unexpected arrived. Not comfort. Not clarity. A voice.

It wasn't audible, but it was absolute. A knowing dropped into me like a stone in still water:

"Life will never be the same."

It wasn't a warning. It was a prophecy.

In the weeks that followed, I moved through the halls of my high school in a haze, numb and hollow. But I kept showing up. That's what you do when you're raised to survive.

One day, I got called to the administration office. I had no idea why. When I walked in, there was a woman, maybe a teacher, maybe a counselor. I can't remember her name, but I'll never forget the kindness in her voice.

"I want to show you something," she said softly.

She opened a door to a classroom. Inside, a group of students were typing furiously. Their faces were focused, their fingers moving fast across the keys. It was some kind of type-a-thon. They were raising money for me to go to Washington, D.C., to represent Florida as a student senator through FBLA, the Future Business Leaders of America.

I didn't know what that meant. I didn't understand why I'd been chosen. I could barely feel anything, but I went anyway. My mother handed me a loaf of bread and a jar of mixed peanut butter and jelly, and I got on a plane to Washington alone.

I remember walking through D.C., surrounded by people in suits, moving with power and purpose, their confidence almost intimidating. I kept asking myself, What am I doing here? Who do they think I am?

It would take me years to find the answer to that question.

The Messages I Was Afraid to Share

By my forties, life had reshaped me more times than I could count. I had rebuilt, recalibrated, and refined. I had faced disappointment and dug deep for resilience. I'd done therapy, attended workshops, filled journals, and prayed until the silence became familiar. And somewhere in the quiet of all that inner work, something new began to arrive—messages.

They weren't just thoughts. They weren't affirmations either. These were downloads. Clear. Direct. It felt as if Spirit had tuned a frequency meant only for me.

They came to me when I least expected it, usually while walking in nature. Unannounced, yet undeniable. I began recording them, almost instinctively. Many felt bigger than me—universal, healing. I knew they weren't meant to stay locked inside my journal.

Then came the nudge—the quiet but firm invitation to share them with the world.

And that's when the fear rose.

Who would listen to me?

What if people thought I was crazy?

What if I wasn't enough of a spiritual authority to carry such truths?

So I said no.

Not out loud. Not to anyone else. Just silently… to Spirit. I turned the invitation down.

And as gently as the messages had come, they stopped.

That silence haunts me more than any mistake I've ever made. Because I know now it wasn't just a moment. It was a doorway. An early call to leadership. And I walked away from it. Not because I didn't care, but because I didn't yet believe in myself enough to be seen.

But life—life is faithful. When you're meant to rise, the call doesn't vanish. It waits… patiently… until you're ready to say yes.

The Unexpected Test: New Mexico State Bar, 2001

It wasn't always the big, planned opportunities that shaped me. Sometimes it was the ones that showed up unannounced, the ones disguised as chaos.

In 2001, I was working in the Continuing Education department at the New Mexico State Bar when everything changed in a single moment. My boss was suddenly escorted out of the building by the director. No warning. No explanation. Just gone.

Two CLE (Continuing Legal Education) classes were set to begin— in twenty minutes. Normally, my boss would make the introductions, welcome the lawyers, set the tone. Now, it was up to me.

The director looked at me and asked, "Can you handle it?"

Every cell in my body screamed: No.

I was comfortable behind the scenes. Standing in front of a room full of attorneys? That felt completely out of my league. I was unqualified—or at least, that's what my fear kept whispering. But there wasn't time to argue with it. The question wasn't *Can I do this?*

It was *What's next?*

So I did it.

I walked into that room, heart pounding, voice trembling, and introduced the course. It wasn't smooth. It wasn't confident. But it was done.

I didn't want to do it again. And yet... something had shifted.

I didn't just step in—I stepped up. I proposed to the director that I take over the department through the end of the year to help recover the financial losses. He agreed.

By the end of the year, I had brought the department's debt down to zero.

That experience taught me one of the most important leadership lessons of my life: you don't always get the luxury of self-doubt. Sometimes, life asks—and you answer.

Not with certainty. Not with guarantees. But with presence. And sometimes, presence is enough.

The Letdown in Houston

In my mid-50s, I'd raised my children, survived a divorce, launched, and let go of a business, and slowly started reclaiming the voice I had long silenced. So when my company approached me with an offer for a management training rotation program—one they had created specifically for me—it felt like a long-overdue affirmation.

It was 2009, and I had been selected for a high-level initiative designed to develop leadership across all divisions and locations tied to DoD contracts. My first assignment? Houston. And not just any project—the Moon mission. The symbolism wasn't lost on me. From the girl who jumped off piers and cracked open coconuts with a claw hammer to the woman being flown across states to help send people to space—it felt like a full-circle moment.

Then, just two weeks after I arrived, President Obama canceled the Moon mission.

Just like that, the opportunity I had been chosen for vanished.

The managers in Houston weren't exactly eager to bring in someone from outside their teams. They had their own people to prioritize, and I became the extra piece—present, capable, but unclaimed. I scrambled to find a position just to keep my job. After all the buildup, it ended in disappointment. No launch. No rotation. No celebration.

It was a letdown—not just professionally, but personally. I had finally said yes to leadership. I had finally dared to believe the timing was right. And yet again, the door that had opened so wide slammed shut.

But this time, I didn't see it as a sign that I was unworthy.

This time, I saw it as a redirect.

Because something else was brewing—something that had nothing to do with corporate ladders and everything to do with soul alignment.

Something that would ask for my whole heart... and give me my whole self in return.

The Deathbed Promise (and the Birth of My Mission)

It's strange how death sharpens life.

When my husband was diagnosed with cancer, everything in me shifted. The worries that had once consumed my energy—career stress, self-doubt, perfectionism—suddenly felt so small. We had five years together, marked by grace, devotion, and the kind of quiet love that doesn't need attention because it already knows it's true.

In the final two years of his life, I became his caregiver. I watched the strong, capable man I loved grow frail before my eyes. And when the time came, I was there—his hand in mine—as he took his last breath.

What broke me wasn't just the loss. It was realizing he had left the world with his dream still inside him.

There were things he had wanted to do. Words he hadn't spoken. Projects he never got the chance to finish. And watching that— watching someone I loved slowly slip away with part of their light still burning quietly inside them—shook something deep within me. It made me face my own mortality in a way I had never allowed myself to before.

If I died tomorrow… what would I regret?

The answer didn't come gently. It hit me like a bolt of truth.

Not sharing the messages. Not answering the call. Not helping women walk their path sooner than I did.

All those years ago, I had said no to Spirit's invitation. I had refused to be a voice, refused to be visible. For a while, the messages stopped. But grief has a way of cutting through pretense. I could no longer pretend that playing small was noble. It wasn't humility—it was withholding. And I wasn't just holding back from myself; I was holding back from every woman who might be waiting for a whisper of her own.

That was the moment I made a new promise:

I would not let my dream die inside me.

And from that promise… something beautiful began to rise.

The Women's Empower Network: A Call I Could No Longer Ignore

It started, as so many sacred things do, with a whisper I didn't quite understand.

I wasn't trying to start a movement. I wasn't planning a launch or building a brand. I just wanted to connect — to create a space where women, especially those who had burned their fingers on life one too many times, could gather, breathe, and remember who they truly are.

The whisper was simple: *"Help women find their voice."*

I didn't feel qualified. Doubt still crept in — days when old stories echoed too loudly. But this time, I didn't wait for fear to leave. I moved anyway.

After decades of helping others in different ways, I had just recertified as a coach and was simply looking for a way to connect with potential clients.

What began as a practical step — a simple way to build connection — became something far more meaningful. I opened a Facebook group and called it *The Women's Empower Network.*

At first, it was just a handful of women — friends, clients, kindred spirits I'd met along the way. We started talking. Sharing. Listening. No filters. No fixing. Just truth — the kind of truth that frees you.

And then, it grew.

Women began showing up from every walk of life — from every corner of the world. Not because I was promoting heavily or promising miracles, but because something in that space felt *real.* Safe. Sacred. Necessary.

What began as a connection point became a living, breathing movement — a vision of women reclaiming their voices, their worth, and their power.

We cried together. We laughed. We spoke the truth unashamedly. We held space for one another. And as the conversations deepened, so did our connections.

This wasn't just a group anymore. It was a sanctuary — a soft place for women to land when they were tired of being everything to everyone but themselves.

And in the process, it called me into a leadership role I hadn't yet seen in myself.

I didn't wait for perfection. I just kept showing up — interviewing women, hosting roundtables, and asking questions like:

What does power look like when it's rooted in truth?

What would it feel like to stop shrinking?

Again and again, the answer was the same: *It would feel like home.*

The Women's Empower Network became that home — not because I had all the answers, but because I was finally willing to stop hiding the ones I did have.

And that's the magic of saying yes to your calling: Source will always expand it beyond anything you could have imagined.

Living on the Other Side of Burnt Toast

These days, I live on the other side of burnt toast.

Not because life has stopped scorching the edges—life still surprises me, humbles me, stretches me—but because I no longer convince myself that the burnt pieces are all I'm worthy of.

I don't eat the toast just because I made it.

I no longer stay in relationships, roles, or rooms that ask me to shrink in order to belong. I don't pretend to be fine when I'm unraveling, and I don't apologize for the fire it took to become who I am.

I choose differently now. I speak up when I used to go silent. I risk being seen rather than hiding behind credentials or perfection. I say yes to the divine nudges, even when I have no idea what's on the other side of them.

That's what living on the other side of burnt toast really means:

I trust myself.

I choose myself.

I don't need anyone's permission to rise.

The Women's Empower Network isn't just a Facebook group. It's the embodiment of every lesson I've learned the hard way. A space where women no longer have to apologize for their brilliance or beg for crumbs of validation—a place where their stories aren't just heard, they're honored.

What began as a whisper has grown into a roar. A living testament that even if the past was messy—even if the toast burned—you can still take your seat at the table of your own becoming.

Because wholeness isn't about perfection. It's about presence. About showing up—again and again—as who you truly are.

And I do.

Every day.

Not because I never doubt.

But because I finally know: the feast was always meant for me.

The Women I Serve (And Why I'll Never Stop)

For a long time, I thought I was the only one—the only woman who mistook attention for affection, who stayed too long, who made herself smaller so others could feel comfortable, who held it all together on the outside while unraveling inside.

But as I began sharing my truth—tentatively at first, then with growing clarity—I realized I wasn't alone. I was part of a quiet, powerful sisterhood of women carrying stories that hadn't yet been spoken aloud.

The women I serve today are radiant. Resilient. Brilliant beyond measure. Yet many don't fully know it. They've spent years on autopilot—performing roles, shrinking to fit molds, building lives around being the strong one, the good one, the giver.

They come to me at crossroads—after the divorce, the diagnosis, the burnout, the quiet ache that whispers, *this can't be all there is.* They don't need fixing. They need remembering. They need someone to stand beside them and say, *You're not crazy. You're waking up.*

In our work together—whether through mentorship, coaching, roundtables, or sacred community—they begin to breathe differently. They begin to tell the truth. They stop apologizing. They start dreaming again.

And slowly, something sacred happens.

They come home to themselves.

They reclaim their voice, their vision, their value. They stop scraping the burnt edges and start preparing feasts—not just for themselves, but for the next woman coming behind them. This work isn't about transactions or keeping score. It's about transformation. Every woman who rises becomes a lighthouse for another. And in helping them rise, I keep rising too.

Leadership, as I've come to understand it, isn't about holding power or standing at the top. It's about being in service—to truth, to Spirit, and to the sacred unfolding of who we were meant to be.

Burnt Toast Truths: Three Lessons I'll Never Forget

If there's one thing I've learned, it's this:

Not everything that's burnt is ruined.

Some of the best lessons of my life came wrapped in discomfort, in silence, in moments I once wished had never happened. But I don't scrape the toast anymore. I've learned to read the burn marks—to listen closely to what they're trying to teach me.

Here are three truths that rose from the flames:

1. Just because it's familiar doesn't mean it's for you.

For years, I mistook struggle for strength. I held on to relationships and roles simply because they felt familiar, not because they gave me life or meaning. I told myself that if I just stayed a little longer, tried a little harder, or gave a little more, then maybe I'd finally be enough. But survival isn't the same as sovereignty, and familiarity isn't the same as truth.

You don't have to keep feeding yourself what leaves you empty.

2. *What looks ruined might carry some deep revelation.*

The things I thought would break me—my trauma at fourteen, the collapse of my first business, the silence that followed when I turned down Spirit's call—were actually hidden innovations to something better.

Every breakdown brought me closer to my core. Every "no" I received led me to a deeper yes.

What looks like failure from one angle is often initiation from another.

3. *You can always make another piece.*

It's not too late.

You are not too old.

You are not too far gone.

You are not too anything.

You can start again.

Make a new choice. Speak a new truth. Create a new possibility. You are allowed to change your mind, change your path, change your story. Burnt toast is not the end.

The feast is still waiting.

The Other Side of Burnt Toast: Final Reflections

When I look back on the journey—from the fearless girl with a hammer and a coconut, to the teenager silenced by shame, to the woman who kept being offered the mantle of leadership and some-times ran from it—I see now that life kept giving me chances to rise.

And every time I said no, life didn't punish me.

It waited.

It whispered again.

And again.

Until one day, I whispered back: Yes.

The Other Side of Burnt Toast isn't just about healing trauma or building a business. It's about reclaiming the sacred within the scorched. It's about refusing to settle for emotional leftovers. It's about rising—not once, but again and again—with your soul intact and your light unapologetically lit.

I used to think I had to have it all figured out to lead. That I had to be polished, certain, unshakable. But leadership—real leadership—is messy. It's sacred. It's deeply human. And most of all, it's responsive.

Now, when Spirit calls, I don't wait to feel ready.

I say **Yes.**

Even if I tremble. Even if I cry. Even if I have no idea what is coming next.

Because I know what happens when you say no.

And I know what happens when you say yes.

This chapter isn't the end of my story. It's a portal. A threshold. A breadcrumb on the trail of my becoming. And if you're reading this, maybe it's a breadcrumb on yours, too.

Because whatever you've been through, wherever you've hesitated, however long you've waited—it's not too late.

There's still time.

There's still room.

And there's still a seat at the table for you.

Even if you've been scraping the burnt parts of your life for years…

You were never meant to settle for scraps.

You were born for the feast.

And it starts with saying yes.

The End.

(But truly, the beginning.)

What's Next?

If you've made it this far, maybe this isn't just my story.

Maybe it awakened something in you—a quiet knowing that you, too, are being called to rise… not in spite of your past, but because of it.

The Women's Empower Network was born from my own journey of hiding, hesitating, and finally saying yes to being seen. Today, it's a sacred space for women ready to speak their truth, grow their visibility, and lead from the inside out.

Whether you're here to listen quietly, share your story, or step boldly into leadership—there's a tier, a rhythm, a doorway made just for you.

Come as you are.

Start where you are.

And trust that it's enough to begin.

Explore our pathways—from community connection to sacred visibility.

Say yes to yourself, and we'll meet you there.

You are not here to wait your turn.

You are here to turn the page.

ABOUT THE AUTHOR
SOL ALÉ JINI

I'm **Sol Alé Jini**. My name means The Light of Truth Embodied. "Sol" reflects light, source, and wholeness. "Alé," drawn from the Greek word Aletheia, means truth and unveiling. Together, my name reflects my life's work: helping women awaken, rise, and live in their truth. This name reflects both who I am and the message I carry into every room — that we are all capable of living fully in our truth without apology or limitation.

As a Spiritual Mindset Mentor, speaker, publisher, author, and the founder of the *Women's Empower Network* and *Pearls of Wisdom by Jini*, my mission is simple: to help women reclaim their voice, embrace their worth, and step boldly into leadership — not someday, but now.

For decades I've studied, practiced, and embodied transformational principles. I blend spiritual wisdom, mindset mastery, and real-world application to guide women toward clarity, confidence, and courageous action. Through heartfelt storytelling and practical mindset shifts, I inspire audiences to see they are more than their past, more than the roles they've played, and more than the limits they've believed.

Through private mentorship, group coaching, live speaking, and my global online community, I create spaces where truth becomes liberating, courage becomes contagious, and women leave ready to take their next step with clarity and confidence.

I'm available for signature talks, panels, workshops, and podcasts that inspire women to own their voice, embrace their worth, and build lives they love. If you're ready to step into your next chapter or want to bring this message to your audience let's connect.

Join the The Women's Empower Network:
www.womensempowernetwork.com

For a free meditation on Conscious Awareness, visit:
www.CoachingbyJini.com

2

YOU CHOOSE HOPE

BY AMY BROTHERSON

*D*o you remember being seventeen? What are the moments that stand out from that time, the best or the worst? For some of us it feels like a lifetime ago. For others it feels like yesterday. Most seventeen-year-olds are excited about what's coming next. They're picking colleges, worrying about grades, building friendships, and planning who they will spend the weekend with, maybe someone they have a crush on.

At seventeen I became a parent, but in a different way than most people mean when they make that comment. My parents' marriage had been falling apart for a long time, and the tension at home was constant. As the oldest of three, a lot of responsibility fell to me. I helped with caregiving and handled many of the household tasks that kept our lives moving.

During my senior year my parents divorced. It was painful and it magnified everything that was already fragile. My father received a job promotion that required him to move four hours away. He had to stay there because he was now supporting two households, his own and ours. The strain of the divorce and of being a single parent was too much for my mother. She had long struggled with anxiety and depression, and the pressure pushed her further down. She attempted to take her life and was hospitalized for several months.

Those months changed everything. I learned young how fragile stability can be and how quickly roles can shift inside a family. At seventeen I was still a kid in many ways, but I had to grow up fast. I learned how to keep going even when the ground under me felt unsteady. I learned how to carry worry and responsibility while still trying to hold onto small, ordinary pieces of a normal life.

I still remember the night we got the call from my father after learning that my mom had been hospitalized. His voice was steady but heavy as he said, "Amy, you guys pack your stuff and go stay with Grandma and Grandpa."

My grandparents lived in the same town, and it made sense. We could still go to school, keep up with our activities, and have some kind of stability. So, I did what he asked. I told my brother and sister to pack their bags.

My brother was fifteen. When I told him, he slouched his shoulders, clearly disappointed. At that age, the idea of living with friends was far more appealing than moving in with grandparents. My sister, only ten, reacted differently. She looked up at me with wide, tear-filled eyes, her voice trembling as she said, "Amy, we lost Mom, we lost Dad. I don't want to lose our house too."

In that moment, my own heartbreak and stress faded into the background. I realized I had a choice. I could follow my father's instructions and move us to my grandparents' home, or I could hold on to the little consistency we had left and keep us in our house.

That moment shaped me. It opened my eyes to the power of choice, how even in the middle of pain and uncertainty, the decisions I made could alter our path. I began to understand that the perspective I chose to carry would guide my actions and influence not just me, but those who were looking to me for strength.

We chose to stay in our home and hold on to as much normalcy as we could. I stepped into the role of caretaker. I made sure the bills were paid, did the grocery shopping, kept meals on the table, and made sure my siblings got to school and church. We divided up the housework, cleaning, chores, even the yard.

I worked hard to keep life moving forward for my brother and sister. My brother stayed on the swim team, my sister continued with her dance classes, and I did my best to keep up with athletics myself. It wasn't easy. There were times when we had to lean on neighbors and friends. I still remember my brother's girlfriend driving my sister to dance class a few times because I was away at a game.

Somehow, we made it work. I kept choosing hope, reminding myself that things would get better, that this season wouldn't last forever. And then, after a few months, we finally got the call: my mom was coming home.

I felt a flicker of excitement. I thought maybe the weight I had been carrying, the constant worry, the endless responsibility, might finally ease. For the first time in a long time, I let myself believe relief was on its way.

When my mom came home, she was doing a little better, but not completely. The anxiety and depression were still there, and in many ways, she was fragile. That meant I wasn't just running the household anymore, I was also helping take care of her.

Again, I stood at a crossroads. I could give in to the exhaustion and the weight of it all, or I could keep choosing to make it work, believing that things would get better. I chose hope. I chose to keep moving forward, even when it was hard. And in time, things did get better. It wasn't easy, I cried my fair share of tears, but mixed in with the struggles were moments of joy and good memories that carried us through.

Eventually, high school graduation arrived. I got into college, then went on to graduate school. There, I began to piece together so much of what I had lived through. I gained a deeper understanding of how powerful it is to choose hope, and how life-changing it can be to have supportive, healthy mentors. I also learned concrete techniques, structured therapy approaches, effective communication skills, and practical tools that not only strengthened my own emotional well-being but could also help others.

My determination grew out of that season of my life. I wanted to help others so they wouldn't have to struggle in silence the way my family did. I came to realize that if children are taught healthy, age-appropriate coping skills, the intensity of their emotional distress as adults can be significantly lessened. And if parents are equipped to support their children's emotions and nurture a healthy sense of self, the ripple effects can shape their children's success for years to come.

As I heard this truth repeated again and again in my classes, it confirmed what I had first started learning when I was seventeen: we have the power to choose. We can choose how we see our circumstances, how we carry our experiences, and how we shape our perspective. And even in the hardest seasons, we have the incredible opportunity to choose hope.

Over the last several years, I've continued to study, learn, and grow with one goal in mind, to help others choose hope and strengthen their emotional well-being. I found my calling in working with children and parents, because those early years are the most powerful time to shape mental health. It has been incredible to witness the changes that can happen when there's even a small willingness to try something new.

Children tend to respond quickly. They're still figuring out how the world works, and when given tools, they can absorb and apply them with surprising ease. Adults, on the other hand, approach change more cautiously. Their experiences and beliefs about the world make them more hesitant, yet with the right support, they too can shift.

Spending countless hours listening, playing, and teaching has allowed me to notice patterns in human behavior, our desires, frustrations, and joys. Again and again, I've seen the same truth emerge: people long for connection, and they thrive when they learn to hold onto hope. Whether child or adult, the thoughts and feelings that rise up during change are often remarkably similar. The journey is about shifting perspective and allowing that shift to influence actions in a more optimistic direction.

Definitions

From my work, I've identified five key concepts that are especially effective in helping people develop hope, resilience, and the ability to change their perspective. Before introducing these five steps, I want to pause and clarify what they mean.

The first is choice. We all know what it means to choose. Every day, we make countless choices. Some are deliberate, but many are automatic, born from patterns or habits we repeat without thinking. The Oxford Dictionary defines choice as "an act of selecting or making a decision when faced with two or more possibilities" (Oxford Dictionary, 2024).

To grow, it's essential that we begin paying attention to these possibilities, and consciously select the ones that are healthier, more positive, and more life-giving. Sometimes that means noticing our habits and interrupting them, even in small ways. Sometimes it means choosing to see our experiences through a different lens. Either way, every choice is an opportunity to open the door to hope.

Next comes hope, one of the most powerful emotional and cognitive tools we have. Many people think of hope as wishful thinking or simply expecting things to get better. And while that's partly true, there's so much more to it. As the Hope Research Institute (2024) describes, "Hope is one of the most powerful tools we have to face life's challenges. It's not just a feeling or wishful thinking. It's an active mindset that can help us move forward, even when life seems difficult."

What I love about hope is that it already lives inside us. Most of us have practiced it in some way, even if we didn't realize it at the time. The challenge is learning how to apply it more intentionally, how to use it as a guide when life feels overwhelming, when emotions weigh heavy, or when circumstances feel impossible.

Then there is resilience, our ability to endure, adapt, and move through difficulties. Many people try to avoid or mask their pain, but true resilience comes from acknowledging it, accepting it, and practicing skills that help us process and move forward. One of my favorite quotes on resilience is from Jodi Picoult: "The human capacity for burden is like bamboo, far more flexible than you'd ever believe at first glance."

That image has always stayed with me. Bamboo bends, but it doesn't break. And when we tap into the power of choosing hope, we too can be flexible and strong in ways we never imagined.

Through my own life experiences, and through watching others navigate their own challenges, I've come to understand hope more deeply. From those lessons, I've gathered and shaped what I now call the steps to hope.

Five Steps to Hope

Step One: Understand Hope

Hope is not a new idea. It has been written about in some of the oldest works of literature and taught by some of the most influential leaders in history. For as long as people have faced challenges, the need for hope has been clear.

But as I've said before, hope is more than wishful thinking. It's not just a vague feeling that things might get better. Hope is the belief that things can work out, even if it takes effort, perseverance, and walking through struggle along the way. Hope doesn't ignore hardship; it acknowledges it and chooses to keep going despite it.

In his book The Psychology of Hope (1994), C. R. Snyder describes hope as having two essential parts: willpower and way power. Willpower is the energy that motivates us to move from where we are to where we want to be. Way power is the plan, the mental road map, that helps us find paths forward and fuels more hopeful thinking. Together, they form the framework of an active, resilient mindset.

Hope is also a skill. Like a muscle, it can be strengthened through intentional thought and practice. We build it by reframing setbacks as temporary, by setting realistic and meaningful goals, and by celebrating even the smallest progress we make. Over time, these small choices turn into patterns, and the practice of hope begins to feel more natural and automatic.

Of course, negative thoughts can show up as roadblocks. They can sap our willpower and cloud our way power. But the more we exercise hope, the more resilient we become, and the easier it is to recognize and move past those thoughts. With practice, hope shifts from something we try to do into something we naturally carry with us every day.

Hope is not only a mindset; it is also an action. It lives in the things around us that remind us of light and possibility, things we can choose to notice and hold onto. Seeing hope in others, in small moments, or in symbols of resilience reinforces our own belief that the future can improve. We bring hope to life by acting on it: by taking small risks, by helping others, and by creating instead of numbing or withdrawing. Each action strengthens the framework of hope and teaches us more about ourselves as we apply it in real ways.

Step Two: End Conflict in Your Life

Conflict is a part of being human, and none of us can escape it entirely. It shows up in our relationships with family, friends, partners, co-workers, and even within ourselves when our choices don't align with our values. But unresolved conflict drains us. It consumes emotional energy, damages relationships, and stalls personal growth. Over time, lingering conflict can create not only stress and anxiety, but also physical health problems.

When we release conflict, we make room for peace of mind, clarity, and the ability to focus on what matters most. Even small conflicts can distract us from hope, stealing mental space and keeping us stuck in cycles of frustration or resentment.

Ending conflict doesn't mean ignoring it or pretending it never happened. It means working through it, choosing empathy, patience, and accountability. It means deciding not to let bitterness rule our thoughts. Sometimes resolution looks like reconciliation, and sometimes it looks like inner peace, even without agreement. Either way, letting go of conflict allows hope to flourish.

An article from Psychology Today outlines the main reasons conflict arises. The top cause is ineffective communication, while another common reason is differences in priorities or expectations (Lewandoski, 2021). Learning to adjust, listen, and better understand others' perspectives can greatly improve our ability to resolve conflict.

There are practical ways to end conflict: choosing calm over chaos, communicating clearly and honestly, letting go of the need to win, setting boundaries, forgiving, apologizing, seeking resolution rather than perfection, and leaning on support when needed. You don't have to handle everything on your own. A support system, friends, family, or a mental health professional can help. And even if others aren't willing to move past the conflict, you can still find peace in your own actions and choices, keeping hope alive.

Step Three: Increase Self-Awareness

Self-awareness is a term you've likely heard in therapy or personal development, but it's worth defining clearly. It's not selfishness or conceit. Instead, it is the practice of paying attention to yourself, your thoughts, feelings, and behaviors, and understanding why you do what you do, including the little quirks and habits that make you unique (Cherry, 2024).

Developing self-awareness begins with noticing your thoughts and emotions as they arise, observing them without judgment, and identifying patterns that shape your actions. Journaling can be a powerful tool for this, helping you track triggers, habits, and reactions. Seeking honest feedback from trusted others also fosters growth and understanding.

By increasing self-awareness, you gain insight into how your perspective is formed and how it can shift. Awareness is the first step toward making intentional choices, strengthening hope, and responding to life with clarity rather than habit.

A personal example of self-awareness came when my husband started reading his grandmother's journal. Through her words, he learned a great deal about her life and personality. But what impacted our family most was realizing that her mindset, values, and beliefs had been passed down through generations. Like in many families, some of these inherited patterns were helpful and nurturing, while others were harmful or limiting. Recognizing these patterns allowed us to make conscious choices to change or improve them for our own family.

This experience inspired me to reflect on my own parents and grandparents. It deepened my understanding of why I think and act the way I do, and why I parent the way I parent.

There are many ways to build self-awareness. Personality assessments, noticing emotional triggers, intentionally spending time alone, setting goals, observing body signals, and seeking guidance from a mental health professional can all help. The key is that self-awareness gives us the opportunity to choose, to actively change how we live our lives. Regular reflection on whether our thoughts, actions, and behaviors align with our values and goals helps us course-correct and move closer to the life we want to create.

Step Four: Generate Improvement Strategies

Once you understand yourself, the next step is to develop strategies to improve your mindset, thoughts, and behaviors. Improvement strategies can take many forms. They might include habit stacking, using natural life transitions to build positive momentum, setting and achieving SMART goals, improving communication skills, or practicing financial planning.

Strategies can be simple or complex, tailored to your needs and goals, but the purpose is always the same: to help you choose hope and create a life you value. As a clinician and coach, I work with clients to identify the strategies that fit their unique circumstances, helping them turn intention into action and fostering measurable, meaningful growth.

A strategy I've found effective for nearly everyone is increasing active listening. This approach helps in two key ways. First, it allows you to better understand those around you and form deeper connections, especially in important relationships. Second, it makes you more aware of your own emotional reactions, biases, and assumptions, which helps you respond thoughtfully across all areas of life. Healthy, trusting relationships are essential for personal growth, and active listening strengthens these connections by making people feel truly seen and heard.

Active listening also teaches patience and mindfulness, skills that improve how we manage emotions and reactions. When we listen fully without jumping to conclusions, we're able to consider new perspectives, broaden our thinking, and reduce defensiveness. By hearing others well, we are more likely to receive honest feedback, which is essential for learning and growth. Understanding a situation fully before reacting leads to better decisions and fewer impulsive choices.

I've seen active listening transform relationships, both marital and parental. While it can feel awkward at first, it consistently increases relationship satisfaction and fosters a greater sense of self-worth

(Bodman et al., 2022). Strategies like this make choosing hope more attainable. There are many resources available, from therapists, coaches, and self-help experts, but it's important to select strategies from credible sources and use proven techniques to feel confident in your outcomes.

Step Five: Find Joy and Expect Miracles

The final step is to seek joy and remain open to miracles. Joy is all around us, waiting to be noticed, and it can be found both in the world and within ourselves. But to see it, we must be willing to look.

One powerful practice to cultivate joy is developing a strong heart-brain connection. The heart and brain work together in ways we're only beginning to fully understand. Research from the HeartMath Institute (2024) has shown that the heart contains ganglia and neurotransmitters similar to those in the brain. These systems communicate back and forth, helping the body respond to stress and challenges in a healthy, efficient way.

One way to strengthen the heart-brain connection is by practicing presence, focusing fully on the current moment. Notice the sounds, sensations, and smells around you. Allow yourself to be completely aware of your surroundings. This mindfulness clears your mind and centers your focus, opening the door to notice joy in even the smallest moments. With the heart and brain aligned, we can improve our overall well-being and better recognize the miracles already present in our lives.

Finding joy and expecting miracles doesn't mean ignoring difficulties. It means creating space for wonder, gratitude, and hope, even in the midst of challenges. By seeking joy intentionally and noticing the everyday miracles, we strengthen our ability to live fully, respond resiliently, and embrace life with an open heart.

Once you find joy, take time to express gratitude for it. Reflect on the things in your life that deserve appreciation. For me, joy comes from the silly things my children do, the progress my clients make, music, small acts of kindness, and countless other moments. Consciously appreciating these things helps shift our thoughts and cultivate a more hopeful mindset. Gratitude opens the heart and trains the brain to notice abundance rather than lack. It also nurtures a belief that incredible things are possible. Expecting miracles isn't about being naive, it's about staying open to possibilities that haven't yet revealed themselves. Too often, we imagine miracles as grand or extraordinary, unearthly power, angels, or instantaneous change. While miracles can be those things, more often they are simpler.

A miracle might be seeing a change that once felt impossible, experiencing a shift of heart or mind, or receiving help from an unexpected source. These small miracles become more available to us when we expect to notice them or invite them into our lives. We can prepare ourselves by imagining our desires as real, speaking life into our dreams, and clearly defining what we see, feel, and want. When we know what we hope for in detail, we become more open to recognizing and receiving the miracles around us.

Conclusion

At seventeen, I had no idea that the choices I made, driven by necessity, love, and sheer determination, would lay the foundation for a lifelong journey of healing, purpose, and hope. What began as survival evolved into a passion for helping others navigate their own challenges with grace and resilience. Every experience taught me that hope is not passive. It is powerful, practical, and transformative when paired with intention and action.

The five steps outlined in this chapter, understanding hope, ending conflict, increasing self-awareness, generating improvement strategies, and finding joy while expecting miracles, are not abstract ideals. They are lived truths, choices available to anyone willing to take them. You don't need perfection. You only need willingness. With each small step, the path toward a more resilient, meaningful, and hopeful life becomes clearer.

Hope does not erase pain. Instead, it equips us to move through it. It gives strength when life feels unbearable and perspective when darkness threatens to take over. Most importantly, it reminds us that we are never truly stuck. No matter where we are, there is always another choice, another step, and another opportunity to believe in something better.

So, whether you are seventeen or seventy, remember this: hope is already within you. As Christopher Reeve once said, "Once you choose hope, anything is possible." I believe this wholeheartedly. When we consciously choose hope, we unlock new possibilities. The key is simple: choose it, and keep choosing it, one moment at a time.

References

Bodman, D.; Van Vleet, B.; Day, R (2022) *Introduction to Family Processes: Diverse Families, Common Ties.* Routledge

Cherry (2024,n.d.) Boosting Self-Awareness.
https://www.verywellmind.com/self-improvement-4157212

(2024) Oxford Dictionary
https://www.oed.com/search/dictionary/?scope=Entries&q=choice

Hope Research Institute
https://www.hriaz.com/our-mission-1

Lewandoski Jr., Gary W. (2021, June 10). The 10 most common sources of conflict in relationships.
https://www.psychologytoday.com/us/blog/the-psychology-of-relationships/202106/the-10-most-common-sources-of-conflict-in-relationships

Snyder, C.R. (1994) *The Psychology of Hope: You can get there from here.* Free Press

(2016) *Science of the Heart: An overview of the research conducted by the Heartmath Institute.*
https://www.heartmath.org/research/science-of-the-heart/

ABOUT THE AUTHOR

AMY BROTHERSON, LCSW, MSW

Amy Brotherson, LCSW, MSW is a clinical social worker, instructor, author, and motivational speaker. Her real-world experience allows her to connect with and educate individuals of all ages. Through years of study and meaningful experiences, Amy has developed a unique and heartfelt perspective on adversity, strength, and compassion.

Her background in Social Work, Psychology, and Behavior has equipped her with practical methods that make it easier to understand why people do the things they do. With this understanding, lasting change becomes possible.

Drawing from years of working with individuals and families, Amy has now expanded her work into the business world, driven by her passion for helping more people recognize and use their strengths to improve both their personal and professional lives.

Connect with Amy:
www.hilltopcounselingservices.com
www.youchoosehope.com

3

LUCKY TO BE RETIRED

BY ANN-MARIE LORDE

*H*i, my name is Ann-Marie, and I will be taking you on a journey of navigating change. This chapter reflects a deeply personal season in my life, when doors closed in ways that were both painful and life-changing. The first was the death of my husband, and not long after, less than three months later, I retired from my high-paying job. Those two changes shook my foundation. What I share here are the tools I developed to help me remain steady and move through these changes successfully. My story will be told through a series of frames and gates.

A picture frame has four sides, and our life stories can also be viewed through the lens of a camera and displayed in a frame. Each moment, each chapter, becomes an image that we carry with us. Imagine a photographer or even a teenager with a phone capturing the movement and daily rhythms of people in ordinary places: rushing through an airport on the escalator, climbing the stairs at a mall, or stepping into an elevator to go up or down.

Those people, in many ways, reflect life itself. Some are moving upward, some downward, some stepping aside for a while, and others choosing the harder, slower climb on the stairs. Some take shortcuts, some linger, and some never stop moving. Each decision, each path, and each choice can be framed like a picture shaped by the perspective of the one holding the camera and influenced by their own experiences and environment.

Consider a wheel with all its cogs turning in rhythm, offering another perspective on how we can examine life itself.

Each cog represents a cycle, and as the wheel keeps moving, it carries us through these cycles: order shifting into chaos, then chaos slowly returning to order, harmony giving way to disharmony, and disharmony returning to harmony. This is the rhythm of life, and none of us are exempt from it.

We must allow ourselves to be uncomfortable and feel the weight of that discomfort for healing to begin. Any moment of disconnection is not random; it is your compass pointing you toward what is imbalanced within.

In those moments, the best thing we can do is stand still, quiet ourselves, and listen. Only then can we begin to identify the true source of our unrest. That is the path toward recalibration, the way back to balance, and the way to restore perspective within the cycles of our lives.

These cycles remind us constantly that our lives are never fixed. We are always moving, flowing, reshaping. Perspective, much like life itself, is never static. It is fluid, changing with time and circumstance. The way we see the world is influenced by two key elements of our surroundings: the nature of the environment around us and the environment in which we were nurtured. Both leave lasting marks on how we think, feel, and live.

The way we approach life, then, is shaped by perspective. Any true change in perspective begins with awareness; awareness of these two elements and how they influence us as individuals. With that awareness, we gain the power to shift our perspective, to reinvent ourselves, and to become better versions of who we are, all through the strength that already lies within.

Perspective shapes our resilience and our strength to move through the waters of life. At every step, we are called to pause and question ourselves: Are my actions guided by who I truly am, or by how I was nurtured and programmed to be?

When we dare to ask these questions, we are confronted with our past. We begin to take responsibility for our existence and for who we have become. We start to recognize the patterns in our lives—the repeating cycles that either carry us forward or keep us bound. And if we choose, we can make a conscious effort to change, to grow, and to transform into a better version of who we are and who we can become.

Change, however, is never mandatory, it is always a choice that we make. The people around us may never change, and even we may remain the same if we do not take actions. Yet, within us lies the power to decide who we will become or not. We can choose to be stronger, more resilient, a visionary, an extraordinary being.

To walk this path of transformation, one thing is essential: we must believe in ourselves. More than that, we must love ourselves enough to keep striving toward the better version of who we are today.

Considering the two elements of the environment that shape our perspective, how then do we find our voice and vision and draw strength from within? It always circles back to change. Change can be embraced as a new beginning, or seen as looking at a recurring situation through a different lens. Each morning we rise, we are given that chance again. Every day is a new beginning. Every change is an opening, a gate through which we can step. And in that space, we hold the power to choose, to reframe, retrain, reprogram, and reinvent. These are the four Rs, the frame that shapes the picture of the new you.

The first R is reframing. It begins with the present moment, who you are right now. Not the past, because the past is already gone. Not the future, because it may never come to pass. It starts here, in the now. To begin, I invite you to try a mirror exercise. On a scale of one to ten, ask yourself three questions. Let them be about something you feel deeply about, something you are passionate about, or something you know well. Be honest with yourself, radically honest. Approach this exercise with an open heart and an open mind. Before you begin, pause for breath. Quiet the noise inside your head, the restless chatter of the mind that leaps from thought to thought like a monkey. Breathe, still yourself, and let the truth rise to the surface.

EXERCISE 1

When you are ready to begin, sit in front of your mirror in a quiet place where no one will disturb you. Take a deep breath, counting to four as you inhale. Hold it for another count of four, then exhale slowly to the count of six. Repeat this three times or more, whatever feels right for you. As you breathe, allow whatever thoughts come to the surface, acknowledge them, and then let them go.

When you feel ready, look into your own eyes in the mirror. Say to yourself, slowly and with meaning, "I love you, me," three times. Then pause. Let the words sink in until you feel a small sense of ease in loving yourself. From this space of honesty and openness, ask yourself the following questions:

What do I know about my passion or my area of expertise?

What do I know that I do not know about my passion or my area of expertise?

What do I not know that I do not know about my passion or my area of expertise?

Be truthful with yourself as you answer these questions. Do not try to give the response you wish were true. Let it be raw, even uncomfortable. When you review your answers, you should notice a shift within. You should see yourself, your passion, your expertise, from a new angle. The question quietly arises: How much do I truly know and understand?

This reflection can stir deeper awareness. You might begin to recognize where you are in your journey, how your choices have been shaped by the way you were nurtured, the culture you grew up in, and the lessons life has taught you. If you are completely honest, you may find that your answer to the third question is very small, maybe only a one or two. But that is not failure, it is the beginning of a wider path of discovery.

With this shift in perspective, ask yourself: can I nurture a different way of thinking to bridge the gap between where I am and where I want to be? Or am I standing here, whether in success or failure, because of the choices shaped by the environment in which I was raised? For some, this may not be easy, it is, after all, a foundational exercise. Yet it is necessary for framing the picture of your newly reimagined self.

You have reached the first gate to change, one that has been thrown open for you. What will you do? Will you step through, take a step back, or stay rooted in place, becoming a relic of the past? Moving forward comes down to choice, and the courage to act despite fear. Walking through this first gate requires an open mind and a willingness to leave the past behind. The longest journeys always begin with a single step.

Once you take that first step, go all in. Follow through and see where the path leads. You will notice shifts in your thoughts and emotional responses, a newfound inner strength, and a resilience that shields you against the chaos of the world around you.

As your perspective continues to shift towards the new you the next side of the picture frame to be slotted into the groove will be to retrain and retool yourself. Retraining is a process that begins with accepting that we cannot know everything about ourselves, and as we work on our reframing we will begin to see where we need to add value to our arsenal of tools and move towards the second gate of change. As with reframing, we must approach retraining with an open mind, an open heart and open ears paying attention with openness to the detail of what the next step will be. Carefully assessing the detail and the fine print of your life. Now that you know that what you do not know about your passion or area of expertise is wider than you think, how do you add value to become a bigger better version of you, how do you expand your vessel so that you can grow and expand your mastery. This exercise will be a free flow exercise, make sure you have a writing pad and a pen nearby.

EXERCISE 2

When you are comfortable to proceed with the second side of your picture frame, find a quiet place where you will not be disturbed. Take a deep breath to the count of four, hold to the count of four and exhale to the count of six. Repeat three times or more acknowledging whatever thoughts come and let them go. When you are ready to begin, divide the page into three columns and begin by asking yourself '*What are the top three tools that I need to support me becoming a bigger and better me?*' Jot down what comes to you. The next question you ask will be '*What are two additional tools that I will need to add value to my mastery.*'

This exercise will call for you to trust your intuition, there are no right or wrong answers, it is a list that can change or expand as you sit with it. When you look at what you have jotted down, decide if you need to change it in any way by deleting any tool or expanding the list. In the second column explore if the tools you have listed are going to be a retooling exercise, an upskilling exercise, or learning something that is totally new.

The third column is where you will take the first step out of your comfort zone, where the impetus to change will occur, where you are challenged to face your fear of change. If it is a retooling exercise, what will be the purpose of the exercise? Is it to improve who you are or what you do or is it to repurpose how you work and interact with yourself and your clients. If it is going to be an upskilling exercise, is it an upgrade to your existing skills, are you adding a new skill in your area or expertise, how will this new skill add value to your development? As you carefully review this exercise, do not be afraid to embrace that this area of expertise that has served you for many years is no longer for you and it is time to step into something new and chart a totally different path. Be resilient enough to learn a new skill that is outside of your comfort zone, challenging your boundaries of existence, creating a new stage for you to shine on.

Realistically speaking this will call for creating new habits, whilst at the same time you may have to remain in your old scenario to springboard into the new. Only you will know and understand your circumstances. Moving forward will call for inner strength and trusting your intuition. Creating measurable goals at every stage to assure your success and not being afraid to revisit these goals to ensure they still meet the vision you have created for yourself and your success. Where failure occurs draw on your inner strength and resilience to face the failure and see it as an opportunity to improve and grow stronger.

The third side of the picture frame will be the reprogramming of your subconscious mind. It is said that our thoughts create our reality, and our reality is created through three levels of consciousness—consciousness, subconsciousness and super consciousness. Our thoughts when driven by strong negative emotions will have a negative impact on us and by extension our environment. The intention of our reprogramming here is to drive positive change through mastery of the self by recognizing the weight of limiting beliefs you may carry. Working through your limiting beliefs helps you replace them with new, empowering thoughts that inspire positive behaviors and attitudes. As you do, you gain greater control of your life and the confidence to make choices that truly align with you.

This exercise can be an emotional one, you may cry, you may laugh, you may be angry, you may even have negative thoughts about yourself or others. We will not be acting on these emotions. We will be tapping into our memory banks, where the weeds reside and where the memories driving your limiting beliefs are stuck. You will need a pad and pen for this exercise.

EXERCISE 3

When you are comfortable to proceed to the third side of your picture frame, find a quiet place where you will not be disturbed. Take a deep breath to the count of four, hold to the count of four and exhale to the count of six. Repeat three times or more acknowledging whatever thoughts come and let them go. When you are ready to begin, divide the page into four columns—the first column is your limiting belief, the second column is the source of the limiting belief, the third column is why must I reframe this limiting belief, and the fourth column is the new affirmation.

Identify one limiting belief from the following areas of life—your health, money and relationships. The first thing you will note as you begin to identify these limiting factors is the level of deep emotion that is attached to them. When you examine the emotion that has led to these limiting beliefs it would have been triggered by something traumatic, something negative. The classic one around money that we will see referenced very often is 'money is the root of all evil'. An example of a limiting belief scenario around relationships could be pleading with your dad or mum not to go on vacation and leave you with grandma, and after they leave you are inconsolable, and you cry until you drift off to sleep. They return and you are happy again, but that negative emotion has taken root. This incident can trigger abandonment issues as an adult where you may refuse to go on vacation and leave your children even though you are aware that they will be well taken care of by their grandparents. How would you reframe these two limiting beliefs to positive affirmations?

As you complete this exercise, be respectful of the fact that our emotions can have a negative or positive impact on our environment, and visa versa. Our emotions are in constant motion, because of this when we approach our third gate of change, we must have clarity as to what our future self should be, returning to what truly matters, and not creating chaos in our lives because of lack of clarity. Clarity of awareness is where we are reinventing ourselves to be the best version of ourselves.

Reinvention is the call to action for yourself to become the new you. This is where, by design you trust, surrender, show up with heart and align to your authentic self. Reinvention completes our picture frame. By embracing the gates of change we build our strength and resilience by saying yes to the opportunities that present themselves to us, putting us squarely into the thick of things. Our final exercise will be a very simple one that will compel us to accept the call to action to reinvent and transform ourselves into extraordinary individuals. Your pad and pen should not be too far from you.

EXERCISE 4

With this exercise we are going to harness the energy of the sun and ground ourselves by walking barefoot on the grass. Take a few deep breaths while lifting your face to the sun with your eyes closed and say, '*Father Sun Mother Earth I have now completed the reinvention of myself, my transformation into an extraordinary person, a better version of who I am.*' Assert this statement with belief, feel the emotions of the new you. You should feel the energy of Father Sun and Mother Earth flowing through your body, an energy shift. Think about five rituals that you will complete every morning to honor yourself and to bring clarity to your day. Make a list of rituals that will get you going in the morning, they do not need to be elaborate— they can be as simple as brewing and drinking your first cup of coffee, stretching, breath work, mediation, journaling, listening to music, feeding the birds, walking on the beach or near water, walking in nature, hugging a tree. All simple but very powerful rituals.

As we complete these four simple but powerful exercises, we must remind ourselves that change is to be embraced and not shunned. Embracing change will call for discipline and not efficiency. It is about stripping away the layers of emotion and giving ourselves permission to speak with a voice of vision and strength, returning to what truly matters.

Our first instinct when faced with challenges to our life perspective requiring necessary change will always be to resist and ask what went wrong? If you failed in some way? If you missed something? See it as a time for refinement. The Book of Isaiah 48:10 aptly reads: *'I tested you in hard times just as silver is refined in a heated furnace'*. These four exercises are not only about accepting change and the closing of current chapters in our life, but it is also about us removing the excess in our lives, and what is no longer serving our higher purpose. Learning from and embracing this change can be a slow process, part of our cycles of life that we repeat to carve away what is necessary, until we learn, until we grow. This is a weapon of precision not punishment. It is about building resilience and strength living with less on the inside and out. With gratitude being lucky to be retired with a new lease on life.

ABOUT THE AUTHOR
ANN-MARIE LORDE

Ann-Marie Lorde is an industrial relations specialist and teacher. She inspires her colleagues and students to strive for excellence and to add value to the lives and spaces they touch.

Her chapter, "Lucky to be Retired," explores embracing change as a picture frame by applying the four Rs: reframing, reprogramming, retraining, and reinvention.

She is proud to have published "Migration in the Global Economy: Challenges and Opportunities for Caribbean Trade Unions," in Trade Union Responses to Globalisation (Ed. Verena Schmidt, ILO Geneva, 2007), and "Capacity Building: Preparing Caribbean Public Sector Unions for an Economic Environment in Transition" in Just Labour (Autumn 2005).

Her dream is to become a featured speaker on embracing change and to lead transformational leadership workshops.

When Ann-Marie is not coaching, writing, or teaching, she allows her artistic side to shine forth.

Connect with Ann-Marie:
Email: annmarielorde@icloud.com

4

LIFE BETWEEN THE BOOKENDS

BY BETH GOLDEN

*E*verything in life has a beginning, a middle, and an end. Each of us experiences different chapters, shaped by age, family dynamics, education, work, and the relationships we maintain, in business, home, and life. These experiences reflect the most vital relationship of all: the one we have with ourselves. Within each chapter, we encounter the lessons that define us, and how those lessons unfold between the bookends of our lives.

Some chapters leave a deeper mark than others. With the benefit of hindsight, we see how our actions, or the actions of others, shape the path we take. The most significant chapters are often those that push us in an entirely new direction, forcing us to navigate uncharted waters.

At its core, life is about two things: Change and Relationships. Change is inevitable. In fact, when we're done changing, we're done. Yet, we often resist change by kicking, screaming, and complaining, until we finally settle into a new reality. Equally, relationships hold a powerful role in shaping who we are. The connections we form with others are essential to our growth. We are social creatures, and loneliness can have devastating effects on the flow of life. And the most surprising truth? Relationships are all about change, too!

There are moments in our lives that become defining turning points. These moments are often sparked by unexpected changes in our relationship statuses. Many times, these changes can feel overwhelming, sometimes even traumatic. It might come from the death of a loved one such as a parent, grandparent, spouse, child, best friend, or beloved pet. Or it could be the fallout of a divorce that upends your life, turning it upside down in an instant. It might even be the shock of being laid off, throwing you into a world of uncertainty and financial stress.

The first impactful chapter of my life launched me on a new path, one that took three years to catch up to. There were many times during those three years when I believed I was okay, only to be jolted back to the reality that I wasn't quite there yet. But as I eventually found solid ground beneath me, this deeply traumatic experience guided me toward a direction that was far more aligned with my soul's true purpose and my deeper contribution to humanity.

The first impactful chapter of my life was unexpected and had a clear beginning, middle, and end.

This is a raw and intimate recounting of a pivotal moment in my life, an event that shattered the timeline of my existence, that I thought was on solid ground. I was married and a stay-at-home mom to two teenage sons. Life was full of hectic school and sports schedules, and all the little things that made up the rhythm of our daily existence. We were happy, and the boys seemed to be in a good place. My husband and I had been married 15 and a half years, and we had settled into a comfortable routine.

But those first ten years of our marriage were anything but calm. They were filled with angry arguments and hateful moments. We were young, and we had the energy to fight. We both liked to be right, and we would go toe-to-toe, determined to prove our points. We repeatedly fell into a cycle of verbal, and at times, physical abuse. After each fight, I would experience what I now call a "post-fight hanger," a feeling of exhaustion, disdain for his very existence, and a heart protected by a fortress from future attacks.

Time would pass, my fragile heart would soften, until the next volatile exchange. We sought the help of several counselors but none could provide insights into how we truly understood one another or how to honor each other's unique, amazing qualities.

After ten years and a move from Colorado to California, things began to shift. We communicated much better, and for the first time, we figured out how to avoid conflict, maintain peace, and be supportive of one another. We mastered the art of dividing and conquering the boys' conflicting sports schedules. We even started taking long walks every evening, where we'd share how our day had gone. It felt like we had finally found our happy space.

My husband loved riding his motorcycle—his bright yellow crotch rocket. He was always fully geared with a full-faced helmet, protective jacket, gloves, and steel-toed boots. He relished every weekend adventure. He'd ride the twisties through the mountains with a group of his riding buddies. There was one vacation when the boys and I drove several hours to a beautiful ski resort. My husband rode the motorcycle. We'd reconnect at rest stops and make sure he was okay. He loved it, and so did we, watching him in his element.

He worked in IT, and he was damn good at what he did. By this point in our marriage, I worked part-time at a community college. Once a month, on a Tuesday, I stayed late to take notes for a specific committee meeting. On those days, I didn't get home until after 4 p.m. My husband was supposed to stay with the boys at home until I got back.

But one Tuesday, when I arrived, he wasn't there. He'd left me a text saying he was hanging out with his boss for a bit. I didn't think much of it at first, because sometimes he'd get caught and lose track of time. But as the clock kept ticking without his arrival, I began to feel the first stirrings of frustration. I texted him, but no reply. By 6:00 p.m., I had to leave to take our son to youth group while I kept texting still without response. It wasn't the first time he'd lost track of time, but it was often enough that I had started to feel that familiar knot in my stomach.

I was beginning to get both angry and anxious. I picked my son up from youth group. It was now 8:00pm.

It was about 9:00 PM when I heard the knock at the door. Hmmm, I remember thinking, It's kind of late for a random visitor. When I opened the door, I was greeted by a female police officer. In that moment, many thoughts raced through my mind at lightning speed. I quickly took inventory: The boys are home and safe. Not once did I think the knock had anything to do with my husband.

She asked if I was Mrs. Wade, and I nodded, yes. Then, the words that followed sent a chill through my body and instantly threw me into an adrenaline-fueled daze. These were her words: "I'm sorry to inform you that your husband has died due to a motorcycle accident. I was able to find you because he had a receipt with your address in his pocket." She held up a gallon Ziplock bag containing the receipt, his watch, and his wedding ring. She mentioned that his wallet hadn't been found at the scene.

In less than a second and the blink of an eye, my world changed. The officer was gentle, kind, and her voice filled with empathy. She asked if I wanted her to stay while I told the boys. I thought the image of a police officer would forever be seared into their minds... like something that would haunt them forever. So, I declined her offer of support.

Time seemed to splinter. When thrust into a new reality, it's as if you're being physically pulled forward, yet your body hasn't quite caught up with the shift. The hardest thing I've ever had to do was tell my sons that their father had died. I had to say it twice, as my younger son was asleep when I first received the news. I didn't want to wake him with such devastating information. He was just a month shy of twelve, and my older son was fourteen at the time.

The next several weeks were a blur. I experienced heartache, shock, sleepless nights, and a steady stream of bouquets, food, cards, calls, and loving family, friends, and neighbors. I was keenly aware that I was being held and loved through the pain, though I couldn't fully grasp its magnitude at the time. I was 46 years old, and grief of this scale was something I'd never experienced before.

The weight of that grief was deeply physical. My heart ached, my body felt heavy with sorrow, and a fog seemed to cloud everything. There was nausea, disorientation, and an inability to retain even the simplest thoughts. My body remained in a state of shock for over a month before loosening its grip.

During this time, several neighbors kept an eye on me, walked with me, made sure we ate nutritious meals and drove us to doctors' appointments and the grocery store. One kind soul even took my oldest son and me to view his father, my husband's remains. I didn't want to go; I wanted to remember him full of life. But I couldn't let my fourteen-year-old son face that moment alone. He needed closure—the undeniable truth that his dad had left his physical body.

When I finally looked at my husband, a thought struck me: This is the physical vessel, but not the person. It became instantly clear that we are spirits having a physical experience. Once the spirit no longer animates the body, the person I knew as my husband was no longer with us, at least not in physical form.

I have so many fond memories of people's love and generosity toward me and the boys. I often found myself thinking, *how can I feel so horrible and so loved at the same time?* I understood God's grace, which gave me the strength to extend grace to myself and to my sons. In those early days, I was incapable of doing so many things. It felt strange to me since I had always been skilled at creating order. I had no control. And for the first time in my life, I didn't hesitate to ask for help.

There were countless moments over the days, months, and even years when I convinced myself that I was okay, that I was func-tional. Then I'd hear a song, or a familiar scent would waft by, and suddenly, it felt as though the grief of losing my husband had struck me all over again, hitting me in the head and shattering my heart. I missed being loved. I longed for it—the kind of love that's fun, spontaneous, and shared with a true partner. Instead, I found myself dating, trying to fill a gaping hole in my soul. As you can imagine, that's not the healthiest foundation to build a relationship on.

I had an affirmation I can recite verbatim to this day: *I want to be in a committed, monogamous relationship with a single, straight man resulting in marriage.* I was blessed with the opportunity to date some incredibly kind, handsome, fun, and attentive men. Yet, none of them wanted to be in a committed, monogamous relationship. While I enjoyed the time we spent together, I knew deep down that I was dating players. And despite the fun, I was guarding my heart. I was saying one thing with my mouth, but my mind was screaming, *Protect yourself!*

In the end, the protective voice won. I surrendered. I took many deep breaths, let go, and trusted in perfect timing.

On the very day of the third anniversary of my husband's passing, it felt as though someone stood in front of me, placed their hands on me, lifted me up, and firmly set me down. It was as though a coating of rust had broken off my body. In that moment, I gained instant clarity about three relationships that no longer fit. One was a couple I had spent time with, another was a lover, and the third was my counselor. Within one weekend, I ended all three relationships. They didn't end in anger; I was simply done.

It's as true now as it was then: I was patient, I made excuses for their poor behavior, but once the line of disrespect is crossed, that's it. My heart and mind slammed shut, and we were done!

Before all of this, my career had been in high-tech fields, everything from aerospace to pharmaceutical research, and academic institutions. Whether I was at work or standing in line at the grocery store, people would often approach me for advice or share their worries and stress with me. After my husband's death I chose to leave the workforce and focus on being there for my boys.

I was considering a career move to coaching, as it was in natural alignment with who I was. My sister reminded me that I could simply buy a coaching certification online and start practicing. While that was true, it didn't sit well with me. I lived in a high-tech area with several colleges in close proximity, and I love studying. I used to say I'd love to be paid to research and write. So, I started looking into various online schools. Three weeks later, on April 1st, I enrolled at the University of Metaphysical Sciences in Arcata, California. Eventually, I earned a bachelor's and master's in divinity as well as a Ph.D. in metaphysical sciences.

I studied five days a week, six hours a day. As the extrovert I am, I learned to find contentment in my own company. I was thriving, diving into new concepts, and deepening my awareness and connection with my Spirit being. There were moments when I'd pick the boys up from school and struggle to speak after hours of intense focus. I often went for walks to get my circulation flowing, become grounded, and reconnect with the everyday responsibilities of life.

At 50, I wasn't just surviving, I was excited and proud of my academic achievements. But now, it was time to take the next step: starting my practice. Wow, that entrepreneurial endeavor was an adventure and a huge learning curve. From starting an LLC, finding the right office space, developing a logo, to creating all the necessary written materials. I joined the Chamber of Commerce and threw myself into every networking opportunity they presented. Looking back now, I can't help but laugh at how terrified I was to introduce myself with a 10 or 30-second elevator speech.

During my studies, I was most excited about using music frequencies to induce specific brainwave states. This type of therapy helped accelerate relaxation, clear energy blockages, enhance mental acuity, and improve the overall quality and efficiency of my work. As always, I was divinely guided to connect with someone who used an interactive sound device I'd come across online. She lived in Colorado, and I was in California at the time. Despite the distance, she offered to meet me in Ohio to introduce me to Michael Bradford, the inventor of The Genesis Bio-Entrainment machine. I ended up purchasing the device, and that was when my practice truly began.

That chapter of my life was both deeply traumatic and transformative. It spanned a total of three years; years that reshaped me. When it ended, I found myself ready to embark on a new scientific and spiritual journey, one that felt more aligned with my soul's purpose and growth. The experience had its beginning, its middle, and its end, and it definitely left a lasting impact. I still carry the lessons, the wisdom, and the awakening within me. At last I felt alive, alert, enthusiastic, and excited about the independent life I had carved out for myself.

Yes, transformational change can come from happy experiences, too. Meeting your person, getting engaged, marrying, having children, buying a new home, graduating from high school or college, accepting a dream job, receiving a promotion, or even moving to a new state where you don't know anyone. Each of these experiences creates change. And with that change comes its own set of stressors, often requiring support and adjustment.

The second impactful chapter of my life unfolded more gently. It was joyful and grounding in ways I hadn't anticipated. It began 17 years ago when I met a visionary woman. I knew we'd be fast friends yet had no idea about the profound impact she would have on my life, nor did I foresee that we'd travel life's roads together for many years. Thankfully, this chapter of my journey remains open-ended, still unfolding in beautiful ways.

As I mentioned before, I attended several networking events, some of which were painfully early. Business Before Hours or Interfaith meetings often started at 7:00 am. Ugh, I am not a morning person. But on those days, I forced myself to be. I was simply grateful if I managed to get dressed with my clothes on the right side out, or that I was wearing two black shoes—or at least two shoes that somewhat matched. I'd sip my coffee, hoping the caffeine would help me string together some intelligent conversation.

One morning, driven by curiosity, I attended a 7:00 am interfaith breakfast. We gathered around big round tables, and wouldn't you know it—I had another divine appointment with Dr. Zannah Hackett. Her husband sat between us, and we were so caught up in conversation that we inadvertently excluded him. After a moment, we quickly switched seats. From that first exchange, there was an undeniable connection with Zannah. She told me about an incredible technology that she thought could benefit me, and we scheduled a time to meet at her office.

What Dr. Zannah didn't reveal at that moment was that she was the co-founder of the technology—and the CEO of The YOU Institute.

A week later, I found myself sitting in her office, ready to take an advanced human assessment called The Ultimate Life Tool® (ULT). It was a relatively quick test with 87 questions that took about ten minutes to complete. For a personality assessment, that was lightning fast. As I worked through the questions, I couldn't help but wonder about some of them. Questions such as: Which of these six eye colors is closest to your eye color? Are you tall, or seemingly tall? Do you ever go unnoticed at a party? These weren't questions I'd ever encountered on the DISC or Myers-Briggs assessments. I was curious about what I'd learn from the ULT?

Dr. Zannah provided me with something called a portal, a detailed review of my results projected onto a screen. It struck me how far technology has evolved. Just a few years earlier, all our sessions would have been face-to-face, and Zoom didn't exist yet. As I stared at the screen, I remember seeing a bunch of numbers appear in five different rows. Dr. Zannah used those numbers to reveal aspects of myself with incredible accuracy. It was a bit of a blur, and I found it fascinating.

She told me that we are all as unique as our thumbprints, perfect in our own way. The assessment was based on a physio-metric tool, in contrast to psychometric tools. While psychometric tools like DISC or Myers-Briggs measure what's in the mind and how we perceive ourselves, a physio-metric tool examines our physical being, our body that carries us through life and defines who we truly are.

She emphasized that no two people are alike, not even twins, and that our physical bodies hold a deeper significance that many have failed to recognize. We've lost the ability to truly "see/identify" how much energy we have and what we can expect in terms of behavior and positive communication.

The first row of the assessment revealed our Seven Styles; our natural, physical traits. Each of these styles had a name: Regal, Energetic, Absorptive, Romantic, Sympathetic, Perceptive, and Effervescent. While everyone possesses all seven, the traits with the highest numerical values stand out as our most prominent, defining physical characteristics. These traits go beyond mere appearance; they also reflect distinct aspects of our character.

The second row was called Motivators, and it contained twelve distinct categories. These motivators represent the voices in our heads, the driving forces that guide our thoughts and actions. Each of these twelve boxes contained a numerical value, with the highest numbers indicating the strongest motivators. These motivators act as our internal compass, with one serving as the pilot and another as the co-pilot. They help us recognize our natural gifts and talents, which can influence the kinds of careers or paths that feel most natural and fulfilling.

Some of these motivators have names like: Initiating Change, Creating Order, Monetary Discernment, Aesthetic Beauty, Naiveté, Perseverance, and Power, to name a few. When we pay attention to our two most prominent motivators, life seems to be seen with greater ease, as we align with what comes most naturally to us.

The third row defines our sense of refinement, the things we can tolerate in terms of people, places, and situations. It helps us set healthy boundaries and become aware of how long we can spend time in certain environments before our energy begins to deplete. This row clarifies why some interactions feel draining, and it sheds light on why compatibility issues arise between individuals.

The fourth row represents how we connect with others, how we learn, and how we commit things to memory. There are four communication styles: Emotional, Instinctual, Intellectual, and Moving. Each of these styles is like a doorway to your heart. While we all possess all four styles, the one we resonate with the most becomes our primary way of relating with others.

The fifth and final row speaks about the energy we have to use throughout the day and our perspective of life. It determines whether we tend to focus on what's not working first, what is working first, or if we see both aspects simultaneously.

Yes!!! It's a lot of information, and it's incredibly comprehensive. By the end of our session, I had received a 7-9 page report that has continued to serve me well. It helped me embrace the person I am, with my thick hair, curvy body, blue eyes, and quick wit. I see what's not working first, and how I can shift my approach to fix it. Respect for myself and others is a dominant driving force in my life. I connect deeply with people, plants, and animals. My driving motivations are Aesthetic Beauty and Creating Order. To stay motivated and move through life with ease, I require beautiful surroundings in my home, outdoors, my clothes, my hair, jewelry, and even the car I drive. All of these things contribute to my well-being. I thrive on giving and receiving attention, and I truly enjoy the recognition that comes with projects well done.

Knowing the results of my 7-9 page report, combined with the time spent with Dr. Zannah, gave me invaluable insights into so many aspects of my life, like my career choices, vacation destinations, and even the people I can spend more time with and those I should keep at arm's length. It was eye-opening, helping me understand my sons more deeply, especially since they are so different in so many ways. I also learned something powerful, that women are in charge of relationships!

That report wasn't just a collection of words. It was like receiving my personal operating manual gifted to me, something that gave me an incredible advantage, allowing life to flow more smoothly and with greater purpose.

So, I ask you: Where are you on your journey? Are you at the beginning, the middle, or perhaps the end of one of life's big challenges? How are you managing the new realities that are impossible to ignore? Are you feeling the joy of a happy life stressor, yet still struggling to find your balance? If so, the results of The Ultimate Life Tool® assessment will provide your own personal operating manual, just as it did for me.

So, how can this information transform your life?

1. Your personal operating manual explains and supports the feelings you're processing at the time.

2. Your personal operating manual helps bring awareness to your dominant thoughts, ensuring they are constructive, loving, responsible, and nourishing for your soul.

3. Your Personal Operating Manual serves as a guiding compass for your personal development. It supports you in refining your life strategies and enhances the way you show up for life.

4. Through this manual, you'll discover your natural strengths and recognize areas that need attention . It identifies your inherent behaviors, helps you establish healthy boundaries, and prioritizes self-care.

5. Your Personal Operating Manual reveals what makes you unique. It encourages you to embrace these distinct qualities and honor how important you are.

6. Your Personal Operating Manual brings balance to your thinking. It nurtures emotional stability and fosters optimized performance.

We are all complex, multilayered beings, each carrying varying levels of intensity. Whether we're at our best or in the midst of one of those momentous timeline shifting changes, taking The Ultimate Life Tool® assessment and working with a ULT Certified Life Coach offers more than just a quick fix or temporary change. It creates a partnership that integrates both the heart and the mind, resulting in connection, direction, and a more fulfilling way of life.

I am forever grateful to Dr. Zannah for her friendship, mentorship, and the countless opportunities she has provided for me to shine.

ABOUT THE AUTHOR
BETH GOLDEN, PHD

Beth Golden, PhD, Executive Director of the Y.O.U. Institute, brings a wealth of experience in personal development and transformational coaching. She has served the Y.O.U. Institute for over 15 years and holds a Master Trainer Certification as a ULT Technology expert and TYI Professional Life Coach.

Her personal and business coaching is praised for fostering empowered shifts in individuals by quickly identifying what isn't working while highlighting each client's unique gifts and talents. Dr. Beth believes that life is all about relationships and the way we impact one another. Her clients learn how to honor and understand themselves, their feelings, and their energetic responses to life's circumstances. These insights often lead to stronger relationships in business, at home, and in everyday life.

Dr. Beth is also the author of *Golden Solutions for Change* and its companion guide, *The Soulful 7*. These books focus on staying grounded in times of social, economic, and personal change.

If you'd like to get more information, please contact her at: DrBethULT@gmail.com
Visit her website at www.youramazinglight.com

5

FINDING MY VOICE
IN LIFE AND ONLINE

BY DIANA CONCOFF MORGAN

Finding Strength Through Healing the Physical Body

Growing up, I often felt invisible, despite having bright red hair and prominent freckles. I was shy and introverted, easily overshadowed by my two older brothers, who shared my hair color but not my quiet nature. They were loud, confident, extrovert, and outgoing, much like my mom. Only my dad seemed to walk the same quieter path that I did.

By the age of twelve, I sensed that life had a purpose, that there was meaning to be found, but I couldn't grasp what it was. Why was I here? Why was anyone here?

The Loneliness Behind the Smile

As a child, I learned to smile to earn approval. I laughed even when I felt like crying. I didn't want to stand out. I thought standing out was strange. I didn't want to be noticed. It's strange how deeply you can ache for connection, even in a house full of people.

As I grew older, a part of me longed to be invited in—to feel chosen, seen, celebrated. But the noise around me was louder than my quiet soul. My family's laughter, their stories, their jokes, filled the room while I sat just outside the spotlight, hoping someone would turn toward me and ask, "What do you think?"

That silence inside me grew into self-doubt. Was I too sensitive? Too quiet? Too weird? I didn't know how to be loud enough to matter. Looking back now, I know I did matter, but somehow, I never felt loud enough to truly believe it.

I spoke to myself in a voice that was not my own. It was a mix of criticism and invisibility: *"Don't be so dramatic." "Nobody wants to hear that." "You're not important."* These words became the constant background voice of my inner world. Over time, I began to believe them, and act them out.

Being the quiet one in a loud, vibrant family made me feel like an outsider in my own home. I loved and admired my family. I craved their boldness, but I also resented the way I seemed to disappear in their shadow. I wondered if something was wrong with me for being this reserved. Why couldn't I just speak up? Why didn't my words carry the same weight theirs did?

One experience I'll never forget was with my third-grade teacher. At that time, I was terrified of even standing in front of people, let alone speaking to them, and I had to give an oral presentation. I was so scared I couldn't tell anyone. I stood at the front of the room, clutching my notes, and looked toward the back, searching my teacher's face. I felt her judgment, her stare piercing through me. I froze. And then I ran out of the room. All the way home.

My parents did what they thought was best at the time. They never asked me what was happening with me or how I felt; they simply assumed the class was too difficult for me to grasp. The following year, in fourth grade, I was placed in a class with very low academic expectations. I knew I didn't belong there. It would take me all the way until seventh grade to get myself off that track and back onto the *"smart kids"* track.

I faced these challenges well into adulthood. And it wasn't just school; it was happening throughout my entire life. It took me until I was twenty-four years old to feel willing to speak in front of a group. I somehow made it through four years of college without ever taking a class that required an oral presentation.

That experience shaped me more than I realized at the time. It was one of countless small moments whispering, or sometimes screaming, that I wasn't smart and that my voice didn't matter. When that message is repeated enough, it sinks deep, lodging itself into your bones. It becomes the lens through which you see yourself and the world.

So, I became the one who listened. The one who simply watched things happen. The one who held it all inside. I spoke silently, but screamed inside. And though I've since reclaimed my voice, I will never forget what it felt like to be silently screaming, aching to be seen.

Discovering Myself as a Seeker

It was at fifteen that my spiritual journey began. I realized I was a seeker, curious about the light of spirituality, yet experimenting in the darkness of addiction. I tried to walk both paths, but fairly quickly, alcohol claimed me. Later, food addiction crept in, joining the mix and wrapping itself around my life. Still, I never fully abandoned my spiritual quest. Because of that persistence, I'm deeply grateful I attended my first Alcoholics Anonymous meeting at twenty-one and found sobriety at twenty-three.

From the very first time I used a mind-altering substance, I sensed it wouldn't be the answer. It didn't fill the emptiness inside me—it only numbed the pain for a season. I just wanted to belong, to be seen, to be heard, to be known. That fleeting escape felt like the only way to quiet the loneliness and invisibility I carried with me.

Looking back, I realize addiction may have, in a strange way, saved my life. It numbed the pain just enough to keep me here, long enough to seek help, long enough to rediscover myself.

Higher Education, Deeper Confusion

At 23, I was sober. I had no idea why I existed in this body, on this planet. I was utterly lost. I had just graduated from UCSB with a degree in Spanish and Bilingual Education. Once, I had dreamed of becoming a UN translator. Instead, I became a teacher. That low-paying, emotionally draining, and demanding job eventually pushed me toward Corporate America.

I entered the workforce determined to earn what was considered a "man's salary." I was resolute, willing to work twice as hard just to prove myself, this was the '90s, after all. But that pursuit nearly destroyed me.

Dolly Parton's lyrics from *"9 to 5"* captured my experience perfectly:

"They let you dream just to watch 'em shatter, you're just a step on the bossman's ladder. But you've got dreams they'll never take away…"

I threw myself into work, chasing someone else's definition of success, yet I didn't even know what success truly meant to me. Meanwhile, my health was deteriorating, and I still hadn't found alignment with my spiritual path. I was surviving, but not living.

The First Time My Soul Got Louder Than the World

I remember the moment vividly. My body ached, my breath came shallow, and my chest felt tight as I walked into another high-pressure day at work. Fluorescent lights buzzed overhead, the same thin static that lived behind my eyes. A colleague said something, but the words washed past me, as meaningless. Inside were roaring of voices, clear and sharp: "This is killing you."

That day, I drove home and cried so hard I had to pull over. Tears blurred the windshield and the steering wheel felt foreign in my hands. I sat quietly, in that small, terrible stillness, I knew something had to change. I didn't know how yet, only that I couldn't keep going the way I was.

Whole-Heart Awakening — Reclaiming My Strength

I believe our soul whispers to us — until it needs to scream.

My soul's next message wasn't a whisper at all; it was a scream. It came when I became gravely ill with pneumonia. I now believe it was my subconscious desire to leave this life.

During that illness I had an out-of-body experience. From above, I watched myself — lifeless and pale. A voice, which I now believe was a spirit guide, spoke: *"You can leave now if you want."* For a moment, I considered it. Then a rush of thoughts about my mom flooded me, the unbearable pain my leaving would cause her. I also pictured returning only to face the same lessons again. In that instant I knew: I would rather endure this life, live these lessons, and see them through.

From deep within my soul, a steady knowing settled over me and urged, *"Stay. Your life isn't done."*

That was a turning point for me.

The near-death experience wasn't just a moment; it was a turning point that cracked me wide open. I knew I had to dive headfirst into healing my body, mind, and spirit. This led me to enroll in a Master's Program in Holistic Health Education and Counseling at JFK University—a course I later, jokingly called my "Master's in What the Hell Was Wrong with Me!"

That program was truly transformative for me. It brought me healing, reconnected me with my spiritual path, and helped me understand my purpose for living.

But even after that awakening, I didn't leave corporate life right away. My third and loudest soul message led me to another turning point. One day, my young son came home from school and simply said he hated it. His words hit me like a jolt. In that moment, I knew with every fiber of my being that I had to be fully, completely present as his mother and role model.

I didn't hesitate. I left my job to become a working-from-home mom. At the time, my deepest calling was officiating spiritual ceremonies and offering pre-marital, marriage, relationship, and life coaching. This was my passion, and I decided to turn it into my life's work. I launched Blessings To You Ministry. It was a challenge to get it off the ground, but eventually, the business thrived.

For the next 20 years, I lived in perfect harmony, flourishing both as a mother and a business owner. My son is now a grown man, married with a family of his own, and thriving in his career. The journey continues; I am a proud grandma!

The Hallway Is Sacred: Finding Your Voice in Life's In-Between Moments

For a long time, my life was guided by a powerful inner voice—a voice I've always called the Power Within. It has guided me whenever I was willing to listen. This voice inspired me to create Blessings To You Ministry, a place that gave me purpose, strength, and so much healing for fifteen years. But after a decade and a half, I felt a shift. My vision had expanded, and I knew I had so much more to give to the world. The work I was doing was helping people, but it no longer allowed me to fully express my own evolving voice. It was as if I had outgrown my own beautiful creation.

Through leading countless life-cycle ceremonies, I witnessed something truly profound: the incredible power of love to bring people together. I saw families and friends, despite their differences and all the drama a wedding can bring, set everything aside to unite in love. That healing energy moved me deeply. I felt a powerful pull to bring that universal, love-centered energy to a larger audience.

That's when Whole Heart Path was born.

The vision of Whole Heart Path is a world of compassion and love where all people of all generations are inspired and empowered to connect and share their hearts.

Whole Heart Path, which included Blessings To You Ministry, became a thriving business. I learned how to get to the top of Google, growing my ministry to over 100 weddings a year with a team of six ministers. I had achieved a level of success many people dream of, yet I still felt something greater calling me. I knew I was here to make a bigger impact than what I was currently experiencing.

I've always felt a deep, unwavering passion for helping others find their voice, because I understand what it's like to be invisible. From the moment I found my way out of invisibility and silence, my mission has been to help others feel seen, heard, and empowered.

This passion gave birth to Whole Heart Marketing in 2008. It's a company dedicated to helping purpose-driven people authentically share their mission, their message, and their business so they can make a bigger contribution to global healing.

Really, Universe? Facebook? This is my calling?

At first, Whole Heart Marketing was all about websites, SEO, and email marketing. Then social media arrived, and everything changed. We couldn't hide behind a neat website or a polished blog anymore—social platforms demanded visibility.

For me, that demand felt like an old wound tearing open. It forced me to confront the ache of being unseen and unheard. Every time I thought about showing up, fear tightened my chest: *What if no one notices? What if I fail?* I realized that avoiding social media wasn't just a missed marketing move—it was a lost chance for lives, including my own, to experience more healing, connection, and impact.

So, I took a leap of faith.

I remember the exact day it struck me: I was the *"best-kept secret,"* sitting on a mountain of gifts I hadn't shared. That image cut through everything. That day, I stopped hiding and stepped into my truth as a thought leader, not for the title, but for the work I could no longer keep to myself.

As Tony Robbins says, "Change happens when the pain of staying the same is greater than the pain of change."

Long story short, after wrestling with resistance and wishing social media didn't matter so much, I surrendered. I embraced it. I learned how to be visible online and used that skill to support other changemakers and leaders. Still, I knew I had to step out even further from behind the scenes. My voice needed to be heard. And when I finally spoke up, I didn't just change my life, I helped thousands of others find the courage to step forward, too.

The World Rewards Loudness — Not Always Truth

As I leaned into visibility, I noticed something: the world often rewards whoever is the loudest in the room, whether online or offline, and not necessarily the person with the most meaningful things to say. As a sensitive introvert, that pressure has followed me my whole life. Speak up. Be bigger. Be louder. Be more likable. Even the unspoken messages were clear: you're not enough as you are. They expected me loud.

But what if the quiet voice holds the deepest wisdom? What if the most transformative message doesn't arrive as a shout but as a steady whisper that stays with people long after it's heard?

For women, especially those who are introverted or heart-centered, the demand to fit outside definitions of success can feel crushing. We're told to hustle harder, to push past our limits, to chase visibility as if it were the goal. Yet visibility without alignment is just noise. Quiet doesn't mean weak. Small voices can change lives.

Redefining Success Through the Whole-Heart Lens

I remember the moment I realized we needed a new definition of success — one that honors soul over strategy, energy over ego, and presence over performance.

When I let go of the old model and stepped onto the Whole-Heart path, everything changed. My energy shifted. My clients changed. My business grew — but more important than any metric was the change in me: I grew into myself. There were days I felt scared to leave behind the familiar markers of achievement, and then days I woke up with a quiet, steady sense that I was living from a truer place.

Old Success vs. Whole-Heart Success

Old success measured output and approval. Whole-Heart success measures how fully we show up — how much of ourselves we bring, how honest we are, how kindly we move through our work and our lives. The shift wasn't only strategic; it was emotional and spiritual. Letting this shape my choices changed the way I worked, how I served, and how I rested.

Sacred Media: Using the Internet as a Force for Good

We live in a time of deep disconnection even while we are more connected than ever. Social media can amplify division, comparison, and surface-level noise, but it can also become a sacred place.

Used with intention, social media is one of the most powerful spiritual tools we have. Every post sends a ripple. Every video carries a tone. Every message is an opening to lift what's happening online.

When we show up honestly, when we share our voice, our story, our truth, we are doing more than marketing. We are modeling courage. We are making space for others to remember themselves and to feel safe being real.

That is the work of Whole-Heart visibility. That is the power of reclaiming your voice, both online and in life.

Now It's Your Turn: The Power Is Within You

Your voice is needed now more than ever.

You don't have to wait until you feel "ready." You don't have to be perfect. Let that inner power be the lamp at your feet, guiding you forward. Let your heart lead the way.

Whether this is your first post or the next chapter of your life, I hope my story reminds you that your presence is enough. Your message matters. Your story, like mine, can change lives.

Let's raise the consciousness of social media so we can use it to awaken, uplift, and elevate humanity.

4 Steps to Grow Your Online Presence with Purpose

If you're here to make a real difference, your online presence isn't just about visibility, it's about transformation. Here are four Whole Heart steps to grow your online presence in a way that's aligned, authentic, and impactful!

Step One: Root Before You Reach

Set yourself up for maximum success.

Create your own container; a safe, permanent home for your legacy online. This includes a website, a blog, and an email list. Not everyone is ready for you right now, and that's okay. An email list lets you stay present and connected with people until they are ready for you. Through simple, consistent messages, you can continue educating, inspiring, and encouraging them while building genuine relationships over time.

This is about protecting your work and caring for your story so it can reach the people who truly need it.

Social media is a powerful tool, but you can't rely on it always being there or always staying the same. There will always be a new place to "hang your virtual shingle." If you don't have your own website and email list, using only social media is like chasing a flash mob, rushing from one platform to the next without a steady foundation.

Create a Nourishing Online Ecosystem

Your presence is more than a post; it's an energetic home.

You don't need to play the algorithm game. Build your foundation:

- A soul-aligned website
- An email list to deepen connection
- A rhythm of content that reflects your values

Don't chase trends. Create a digital sanctuary that holds your mission.

Step Two: Speak From the Heart

Create a clear message that reflects your brand.

Your Thought Leadership Legacy is about how you want to uplift, inspire, and transform the world. How will you use this powerful tool, the internet, to bring positive change? What are you passionate about? What stirs your heart and lights you up? These are the opportunities to reach people with uplifting and inspiring messages through your social media.

Who Are You Talking To?

Every time you log into your social media, pause and ask yourself: Who am I really talking to? Who is my ideal client? What do I want to share that will make them lean in with curiosity and say, "Tell me more"?

Remember: the internet is built on search engine optimizations. People are constantly searching for words that match what they feel or need. Your success depends on a clear message written in the very words your ideal clients would use to find you.

What Is the Struggle?

The more clearly you understand and express the struggles your clients face, the more they will trust you. What problems do they speak about openly? And what deeper struggles lie beneath the surface? Give words to their hidden fears, unspoken pain, and quiet challenges. When you name that pain with compassion, they feel truly seen and understood.

What Is the Transformation?

What is the healing? What is the hope? Transformation can take many forms and often happens in small steps. It might be a shift in thinking, a new habit, or the courage to try again. Share these different levels of transformation with them, both the subtle changes and the bigger breakthroughs.

Let Your Message Be a Beacon.

Speak with honesty and tenderness. ***When you tell the truth from your heart, it resonates — whether it reaches one person or one thousand.***

Ask yourself:

- Who needs to hear this today?
- What are they struggling with?
- How can I offer hope or clarity?

You don't need to go viral. Just be real. That's what people are craving, and that's what creates ripple effects.

Step Three: Show Up as Energy, Not Just Strategy

"Bring your Whole Heart Essence to Your Online Presence."

You Are Your Best Lead Magnet

Everything is energy. The aim of intentional internet marketing is to let your ideal clients experience the essence of who you are and what you do visually, through your words, and in the energy you bring as closely as possible to what they would experience if they met you in person.

Whole Heart Marketing means showing up with your whole heart, your enthusiasm, your true energy, and your essence in your online presence. This allows your ideal clients to feel your care, your clarity, and your commitment. They don't just see what you do, they feel *you*.

This is how you stand out and get recognized as the expert and thought leader you already are. Showing up as your true self online is the most powerful use of your time on social media.

Yes, you can get help with strategy, design, or other parts of marketing, but no one else can *be* you. Energetically, you can never be replaced by AI or by another person. You are a unique energy transmitter with your own distinct way of attracting the people who are meant for you.

Your Essence Is the Most Powerful Algorithm

People don't remember polish — they remember presence.

Before your next post, close your eyes, place a hand over your heart, and ask yourself, "What energy do I want to offer today?"

Whole-Heart Visibility is about showing up with authenticity and integrity, not perfection.

Step Four: Create a Rhythm That Reflects Your Purpose

"The Whole Heart Social Media Success Formula"

Create and Implement a Strategic Plan

Over the years, and after working with thousands of clients, I've developed a tested social media formula that helps Thought Leaders and Changemakers thrive.

50% Brand Yourself

Half of your social media presence should be about branding yourself—the human behind the mission. Share your passion openly, let people see your heart, and connect authentically while building meaningful relationships. For purpose-driven entrepreneurs, personal and business messages often intertwine.

Show up consistently: four times a day for 15 minutes. Not to scroll endlessly, but to connect intentionally. Join conversations. Share your story. Celebrate others as often as you celebrate yourself by sharing their meaningful content alongside your own.

Challenge: Each week, find five new people to engage with:

- Active community members
- Message-aligned individuals
- Strategic partners
- Thought leaders and changemakers
- Active networkers

And don't just stop at a follow. Connect on multiple platforms, and let them feel your presence.

Here's how you go about it: Like, Follow, Comment, and Share. And above all, always do this with **CARE**:

- **Connect**
- **Acknowledge**
- **Respond**
- **Engage**

Do all these with intention.

40% Position Yourself as the Expert

Marketing isn't about making the loudest noise. It's about inspiring people to take action on your expertise.

Educate. Inspire. Motivate. Share engaging content that reflects the heart of your brand, and always keep your ideal client in mind. Don't just focus on the "how to"—focus on the "why," "what's possible," and the transformation it will create. Post articles, quotes, videos, and even third-party content that meets the needs of your clients.

Remember: on your *personal* social media, let people see your love for your business. On your *business* social media, let them experience the mission and value you bring.

10% Make Your Offer

Yes, you must make offers. But do it with care. Promote only about 10% of the time. Share free offers generously. Give people a chance to know you before you ask them to invest. Lean more into your business pages, but sprinkle in the occasional personal post too.

Think of this rhythm: **Connect. Nurture. Invite. Repeat.**

Because consistency is not about rigidity, it's rhythm.

- **50% Be YOU!** Brand yourself, build relationships, and share your stories and reflections.
- **40% Position Yourself as the Expert You Are.** Share educational, inspirational, and motivational content that reflects your unique voice.
- **10% Extend an Invitation.** Do so with love and clarity.

Whatever your presentation is, let it be an offering, not a performance. That is how you raise both awareness and make your readers conscious of you.

A Whole Heart Manifesto

I believe...

The world doesn't need your perfection. It needs your presence.

Your voice is your legacy.

Social media can be sacred.

You are not too late, too old, or too invisible.

Healing happens when we show up not polished, but real.

The internet is a mirror. When you reflect truth, it reflects it back.

Your Voice Matters.

Your journey; every scar, every victory, every lesson, everything you've healed, every piece of yourself still unfolding—has value. You don't need to be louder. You don't need to be perfect. You just need to be real. Authenticity is what creates true connection. And connection is what propels change.

I believe your online presence can be a sacred space, a place to serve, uplift, inspire, and even grow a business that reflects the fullness of your true identity.

As my gift to you, I created the Whole Heart Social Media Success Formula Mini Course. This course is designed to help you begin your journey with intention and clarity.

It is made for purpose-driven entrepreneurs who are ready to move from invisible to impactful, without losing themselves in the process. Whether you've struggled with showing up, feel unsure about what to say, or simply want a simple, aligned way to start making a difference online, this course is here to guide you.

In this free mini course, you'll learn:

- How to clarify your message so it speaks directly to the hearts of your ideal clients.
- How to show up consistently in a way that feels aligned and energizing—not exhausting.
- The essential steps to creating authentic content that truly connects and converts.
- A simple system to start building visibility, credibility, and a community with heart.
- You don't have to do it all at once. Just take the first step by getting started.

Let this be your next brave move—from hiding to being seen, from doubt to clarity, from silence to a confident, authentic presence.

Your voice is sacred. Let's use it—together.

ABOUT THE AUTHOR
DIANA CONCOFF MORGAN, MA, HHE

Diana Concoff Morgan, MA, HHE is the author of The Whole Heart Social Media Success Formula™: What to Say, Where to Play, How to Win – Intentional Social Media for Purpose-Driven Entrepreneurs. She is a Conscious Digital Impact Strategist, an international best-selling author, a speaker, and a successful entrepreneur with over 30 years of experience, including building two thriving businesses using the very strategies she now teaches her clients.

Diana is dedicated to helping coaches, authors, speakers, and other heart-centered, purpose-driven entrepreneurs who aspire to make a bigger impact in the world. Her clients often rely heavily on relationships and referrals to grow their businesses, and she has developed The Whole Heart Marketing Strategy to help them increase meaningful connections, cultivate strong relationships, and convert those relationships into loyal clients—using proven, practical strategies that work.

With passion and commitment, Diana has guided thousands of entrepreneurs to grow their businesses. She specializes in training on mastering the art of online communication, networking, and client attraction, teaching not just techniques, but how to connect authentically and make a lasting impact.

Get The Whole Heart Social Media Success Formula Mini Course today and begin creating your online presence with purpose, power, and genuine authenticity.

Grab my free gift:
https://wholeheartmarketing.com/minicourse

Connect with Diana:
https://linktr.ee/dianaconcoffmorgan
https://wholeheartmarketing.com/

6

NOT SO DIRTY LAUNDRY

BY HADASSAH ROSE

*T*used to have a recurring dream at night when I was a child. The dream opens at night with fire everywhere burning everything. Buildings glowed the color of molten lava; their surfaces shimmering like hot coals. People run frantically in every direction, screaming as pieces of the buildings crash to the ground. In my mind, it looked like how Sodom and Gomorrah must have been when it was destroyed by fire and brimstone.

In the middle of this chaos, a huge dragon-like creature appears, much like a T-rex with sharp teeth. It stomps through the streets, thrilled by the fear and destruction it commands. Its presence fills the dream with terror, yet there was something strangely familiar about it, as though it had always lived inside those burning streets.

My sister and I are carrying a laundry basket full of dirty linens, walking towards a laundromat. A bright aura surrounds us and somehow, we are untouched by the chaos all around. We step inside, load the machines, and sit together during the wash cycles. The hum of the machines was steady and unhurried, and somehow comforting, even while sirens and shouts echoed just outside the door.

When the cycles finish, we pull out the linens and fold them neatly into a flawless stack putting them back into our basket. They were no longer stained but perfectly white – the purest white. Then, the dream closes.

I had this dream almost every night from the time I was six into my early teens. For decades, it faded until I began writing this chapter. I'll let you decide what it means as you journey with me, but I suspect that by the end, the meaning will reveal itself: there is a laundromat in the soul, and language can wash away what the world has stained.

I stepped into the helping arts early in life. First, as a reading buddy, then as a volunteer in the learning resource room with special populations. I loved those moments when something that once felt impossible alone suddenly became possible with a little help.

By the age of fourteen, I was spending afternoons at the local nursing home, setting up games and helping to feed residents who needed special care. On my very first day, a resident spit pureed carrots all over me. Even now, I smile when I think of it. Another time, I fed a woman with the softest spirit. She never spoke, but her eyes said *thank you* like prayer. I didn't know it then, but those small encounters were seeds. They fell into my soil and waited for a season I couldn't yet imagine.

While I was learning how to care for others, my inner world was quietly unraveling. My teenage years felt like a storm that refused to move offshore, hovering and pounding until I was worn thin. My nervous system stayed braced, always on guard, because I didn't have the counsel to help me navigate my emotions.

On the inside, I grew hard and calloused, but on the outside, I bent easily because I wanted so badly to belong. I wasn't the smartest, or the prettiest, and I was often mocked for being too skinny, too Indian or for dressing "too nice." By the time I was eleven, I was already working for the extras I wanted, because my parents believed deeply in the value of earning what you could.

I loved fashion and house music, so I sought out jobs where I could lean into my extroverted side, even while I felt so isolated inside. No one asked about my feelings, and I didn't offer them. My inner dialogue circled the same dark and single drain: You're not good enough. That one sentence weakened me, left me exposed, and made it harder to hold my boundaries in rooms that were anything but safe.

One of those rooms was a Yahoo chat group, where a man asked to meet in person. I walked to Tim Horton's wearing a cropped halter top under a sleeveless button-down, with faux leather cigarette pants clinging to my legs. He pulled up in a black Trans Am—rugged, unkempt, somewhere in his late thirties. The car reeked of stale smoke.

At his house, three other men were waiting. As soon as I stepped inside, they surrounded me, joints in hand, blowing clouds of cannabis smoke into my face. "What do you want to do?" the one who picked me up asked.

"I want to go home," I said.

They laughed while mocking me. And instantly, drove me back and dropped me off at the same Tim Horton's where it all began.

A reasonable person might think that would be enough to scare me, but it wasn't. It became the first step in a long, jagged arc of dysfunction, shaped by the quiet belief that if I said *yes* enough, someone might finally accept me, maybe even keep me.

Meanwhile, at home, everything looked solid from the outside. Both my parents worked. They managed to provide homemade meals three times a day. My mother was, and still is, the embodiment of nurture. She supported me in my pursuits, encouraged steps I took, and rarely let me see her upset or in tears. My father, modeled discipline and strength through his religious devotion.

We began practicing Jainism openly and with intensity. Mornings started with prayers before school, and nights ended with three more hours of worship, even when homework piled high. I grew resentful toward God because the demands felt endless, but even in my frustration, I could not ignore my father's sincerity. His faith carved a path toward higher consciousness, one I would walk later, long after I had the words to name what it meant for me.

Like many Indian children, I was encouraged to choose a medical career and landed on pharmacy. My high school offered half-day work placements, and I was thrilled when I learned mine would be at the very hospital where I had been born. On my first day, my preceptor and their assistant handed me a thousand-page drug manual, led me to a small room, and told me to read. No guidance. No conversation. Hours passed in sterile quiet until I was dismissed.

I walked out of that building with a clarity I trusted: I wanted to help people heal, but not like that.

I went back to my co-op coordinator and requested a new placement. That's how I found myself returning to my old elementary school, the same place where I once walked the halls as a reading buddy. Life has a way of circling back, and this time it brought me face-to-face with my gifted fourth-grade teacher, who was now working with students in special populations.

I joined her in teaching children with autism, Down syndrome, ADHD, language delays, articulation disorders, and complex communication needs. Because she already knew me, she gave me room to explore and trusted me with creative freedom. That trust stirred something deep in me. It wasn't just gratitude for the opportunity; it was the kind of gratitude that blooms when someone truly sees your natural ability and believes in it.

At that moment, something shifted. I wasn't simply being helpful. I wasn't just filling a role. I felt alive in a way I hadn't before.

Then, the weight of bad grades fell on me. During my undergraduate, I studied hard but still watched my GPA slip lower and lower. I failed a year, got suspended, and was forced to take time off. During that break, while working at the bowling alley, the owner snapped his fingers, criticised me harshly and embarrassed me in front of everyone. Something deep inside me was shaken. I spoke up calmly and never returned after that incident. It terrified me to break out of my *yes-woman* shell, but in that crack, my real voice finally came through.

The spiral wasn't finished with me yet. At a new restaurant in Niagara Falls, I met the friend who would become my gateway to hard drugs. I never had what people would call a bad trip, but the experiences weren't always easy. The crashes afterward were brutal, every negative feeling sharpened, amplified. I would lie awake at night, thoughts gnawing at me, chewing through my sense of self and my purpose. My boyfriends at the time absorbed the shrapnel of my dysregulation.

I said *yes* to relations when I didn't feel a true *yes* inside me, and each of those half-choices chipped away at my moral compass, eroding my self-respect. To me, saying *yes* meant I belonged; that I was wanted. It was a mask for love, but behind it, my worth was held hostage.

And still, even in that spiral, a sliver of light remained. I returned to school and reached out for help. That was when I discovered I had language processing challenges, the kind that left me blank during exams. Once I learned to study using all four modalities of receptive and expressive language, everything began to change. My grades rose, and with them, my confidence.

I started volunteering with a stroke communication group in the hospital, and there I discovered this brought deep joy in my heart. I felt fulfilled helping people who had lost their voices to be heard and understood again. In that space, something settled inside of me. My focus shifted and was clarified. I was renewed. Communication rehabilitation wasn't just interesting to me; it felt like a calling I could show up for every single day.

When it came time to apply for graduate programs, I gathered references from professors, the program chair, and supervisors from my volunteer work. The professors were honest but careful; the truth of my transcripts tempered their praise. The program chair, however, was blunt and told me flatly to "Quit. You'll never get in. You'll never make it." His words broke my heart and, in the same breath, ignited a fire inside me. My strongest endorsements came from hands-on volunteer settings. I didn't receive the American acceptances I had hoped for, so I enrolled in a speech-language pathology assistant program at a local college. It wasn't the straight path I had imagined, but it was the path I kept walking.

Somewhere along the way, in that stretch, I dated a man who couldn't get my name right. Our first night together was a blur of Jack Daniels shots that set the stage for the quality of our relationship. For six years, we followed an on-again, off-again pattern that never moved toward commitment. Every time I asked for monogamy, I was stonewalled. That relationship became a mirror reflecting the part of me that believed asking for more was the same as asking to be abandoned. It took time to realize that a boundary is not a threat; it is a doorway, a space where two honest people can truly meet.

In early 2007, I suspected I might be pregnant. I took the test during a break between classes. Two pink lines. I texted my gateway friend, telling her we needed an eight-ball and whiskey. She asked if I was pregnant. I said yes. She joked about stairs and a coat hanger. I told no one at home and made the appointment.

A social worker asked me, "What will you feel after you have this done?" "Relieved," I said. No one prepares you for how grief and self-resentment can weave themselves into silence after you terminate the life of a tiny human. I don't write that sentence lightly. It is part of my story, and I honor it by telling the truth.

I finished my post-graduate program, and to my delight, it fed into an American school. With my GPA raised from 2.7 to 4.9, I applied and was accepted. We packed my life into a van, and my best friend drove with me to upstate New York. My father was traveling; we didn't say a proper goodbye. I looked at my mother, tears welling in my eyes, and asked, "What if I don't make it?" Tears slid down her cheek. "I have every confidence in you," she said.

Out of eighteen acceptances, five were Canadians. I was one of them.

During my clinical fellowship year in 2011, I met Pat. She had been hospitalized for encephalopathy with a UTI and was catheterized. Three years earlier, an elective surgery to clip an aneurysm had left her with a hemorrhagic stroke. She could produce only four syllables— "luh, mee, nuh, mau."

When I entered her room, her face was pinched with discomfort. My intuition told me the catheter was bothering her. The nurses checked, agreed, and removed it. Despite her limited speech, Pat had profound whole-body communication. She rejected low-tech communication boards and even a high-tech device when offered. I asked, "You want to talk?" She nodded.

I found a case study that described how syllables could be shaped into functional speech and built a program from it. I warned her that the process would be difficult, that frustration would visit us both. Then, we worked intensely five days a week, sixty to ninety minutes at a time, for six months. We laughed, we cried, we celebrated tiny gains: one consonant cluster, one vowel shape, one word stretched into two.

One morning, I walked into the facility to applause from the nurses' station. Pat had verbally ordered breakfast. It wasn't just skill that made it possible; it was her determination and our shared insistence that language could return. That day felt like stepping out of a laundromat with a warm stack of something I had once believed was permanently stained.

Later that year, I met Peter at Jax Beach. I brought a friend along; instincts get louder when someone safe is nearby. He rode a motorcycle—blue eyes, dark hair—his presence equal parts thrilling and unsettling. We had drinks, went to his place, and later ended up at mine. What began as casual hardened into something permanent almost overnight. He started staying over, leaving for work from my apartment and returning each night. I mistook his constant presence for devotion. I didn't recognize control until it raised its voice. When I pulled away, he erupted; when I stayed, I shrank.

One night, I was preparing a dysphagia presentation, and he had been drinking. He insisted we go for a ride. My intuition screamed no, but I ignored it. I put on my favorite jeans and jacket, climbed onto the back of his bike, and wrapped my arms around his torso. On a back road near St. Augustine, he said he'd tap my hands before accelerating. Instead, the bike surged. My grip slipped, and suddenly I was airborne. In slow motion, I saw him glance back as I floated, and a voice inside whispered, *Relax, or you'll break something.*

I hit the pavement, slid thirty feet, and rolled away from headlights hurtling toward me. I ran a quick cognitive check: name, date, orientation. The seat of my pants had burned away. My hands, feet, and knees were raw with road rash. A hot line crossed my chest where the zipper had branded me. The hospital sent me home with supplies, no debridement. At one point, the pain rose so high that light took over me that I went somewhere without pain at all.

I was incapacitated for twelve weeks, completely dependent on the man who had caused my injuries. He admitted it was his fault, but I couldn't shake the suspicion that it had been intentional. Later, I accepted a job in Pasadena and we moved to St. Petersburg.

At a bar, during a small homecoming with friends, he threw a drink in my face and called despicable names. At home, when I reached out to calm him, his teeth clamped around my wrist. A steady voice inside me warned, *Don't move, or your skin will tear.*

When he finally released me, I quietly gathered my passport, phone, charger, purse, and keys. He ransacked the house behind me. I ran to the car. We wrestled for the keys while neighbors shut their doors. He dragged me back into the house. Finally, I broke free, locking the house door behind me, and got into the car. As I backed out, he jumped onto the hood, cracking the windshield. I accelerated, and he fell.

The next time I saw him, police were present while I packed. He convinced them it had all started with me.

In 2012, I took a travel-SLP placement in Texas. I met an eighty-five-year-old man with aspiration pneumonia and a broken spirit. His wife had fallen and both of them were in sub-acute rehab. Depression kept him bedridden, holding him back from the intensive therapy he needed.

I brought colored markers and paper and asked him for the names of the people he loved and the victories that had shaped his life. I wrote those words in cursive, in bright colors and arcs, and taped them across the blank wall he faced all day.

By the end of two weeks, he was getting up to use the bathroom, joining therapies, and strengthening his lungs. He grew strong enough for the swallowing exercises that moved him from pureed food to regular textures. Sharing his favorite ice cream with me, he said it was that word collage that had turned things around for him. He had remembered that he had something to live for.

In 2013, I accepted a position at a moderate-security forensic psychiatric hospital in Napa. During training, a nurse told us something I will never forget: "Eighty-five percent of women have been sexually assaulted, and the other fifteen percent either don't remember or aren't telling the truth."

Her words cracked open a vault inside me. Memories that were buried deep began to pour out of amnesia and into my conscious awareness. Suddenly, pieces of my past that were locked away came rushing back, demanding to be faced.

In my search for healing, I reached in every direction I could find; meditation, kundalini yoga, psychic mediumship, new-age practices, witchcraft, and plant medicine. I was desperate to understand why my voice always felt muffled and why the choices I made seemed to keep hurting me.

The answers didn't arrive all at once. They came in fragments, scattered insights I had to piece together. Yet one truth kept showing up again and again: everything came back to language – how I used it and how I withheld it.

The medical system had left me jaded. I rarely saw people truly healing, and when my workplace replaced me with the very student I had trained, the disillusionment pushed me out the door. On my final day, I sat with a woman in the later stages of dementia, helping her through a meal. She was mostly nonverbal, but suddenly her eyes widened and she cried out, "It's about the language! The language! THE LANGUAGE!" In that moment, my own eyes opened.

I walked away from speech-language pathology for several years, after completing two short roles; one in a therapeutic day school and another with babies learning their first words. Instead, I immersed myself in holistic nutrition, completed yoga teacher training, and went through massage therapy school. I longed for healing that endured, not treatment that had to be repeated.

I kept breathing through my old pain and had an encounter with New-Age Jesus. I sat and inquired with Him until the root of my silence finally revealed itself. From there, I began teaching about the power of words and the purpose of language as medicine—how the sentences we choose to reinforce can either free us or fold us into something small. The money was little, but the meaning was extravagant.

For seven years, my life was transient. I put my belongings in storage, slept in my car, stayed on couches, and rented rooms whenever I could. Then, in one old house, my health collapsed. I fasted and prayed for seven days, desperate for answers, and discovered I was being poisoned by black mold. I fled the house immediately, but the escape only led me into a healing crisis: three more days without nutrition, drenched in sweat and my mind twisted by hallucinations. I woke only to use the bathroom, repeating to myself, *If Jesus can die and resurrect in three days, so can I.*

On the fourth morning, I opened my laptop, returned to my paused radio show, and spoke the truth about what had been happening to me. A client heard my voice, offered help, and removed my belongings from the moldy house. They even paid for my treatment.

In that moment I understood the power of language. Love arrives, not as a grand gesture, but in sentences and actions.

In 2019, I set out to drive to Sedona for a festival where I was scheduled to teach, armed with only a few hundred dollars to my name. Five cars and seven sister-friends caravanned from Chicago to the desert. I taught a workshop called "Decoding the Language of Fear," and when the festival ended, I found myself without a place to be, so I decided to stay where I was.

With no housing lined up, I reached out to the community, asking for short-term places to rest, and DoorDashed between them. When I had nowhere else to go, I slept in my car. A woman opened her home to me for a few months. She was kind, but when she said, "You'll never find anything better than this," I knew it was my cue to keep moving.

That same night, another woman offered me a room in her home. As I unpacked, I found a notecard in the bathroom with Hebrews 11:1 written on it. That verse had been one I encountered throughout various stages in my life. I saw it as a quiet confirmation that I was being held.

The summer of 2020 arrived, bringing with it an overwhelming and encompassing encounter with the living Christ, a miracle of salvation. I was freed. I joined a project dedicated to raising awareness about human trafficking, and we organized an event that became one of the largest in the world. But the news smeared me, labeling me a "conspiracy theorist." The weight of the slander, the relentless pressure, it all became too much to bear.

I drove into the Colorado mountains, hoping I could just disappear and never return. I found a cliff where I believed no one would hear me or find me for a long time. As I made my way toward that spot for the final time, the rain began. I stepped out of the car and saw a full rainbow stretch across the sky.

"You'll have to do better than that," I muttered. "I've already seen rainbows."

But then, at the overlook, something extraordinary happened. Diamonds seemed to fall from the sky—raindrops refracting the light so thick the air glittered. Three rainbows arched over the ridge, their colors lifting my soul.

Tears ran hot and unrelenting, blurring my vision. I lifted my hands to the sky and whispered through sobs, "Fine. I won't try to kill myself ever again, no matter how hard it gets!"

I went back to Arizona with my heart set on God. I sank deep into the scriptures and, instead of just reading them, I let them read me. The language of the Bible softened the tight knots in my mind and calmed the storms in my body. Slowly, I began to see endurance not as punishment but as a teacher.

The real change came in how I told the story of my life. Was I a victim or a victor, carrying wounds or carrying wisdom? That question reshaped me. My purpose grew clearer: to purify my thoughts, my words, and the way I interacted with others, so I could bring healing in the way I was created to do.

In 2022, I moved to Denver and enrolled in a Hebrew Bible college. The studies sharpened my perception: every word is a choice, every thought a seed, every story an agreement. In my relationship with the Most High, I began to examine my speech more carefully than ever before. I wanted to be a vessel of goodness and truth, one that could serve anyone seated across from me.

My past cataloged evil. But it wasn't just the evil itself that haunted me; it was the realization that in so many ways, I had agreed with it by remaining silent. That's when the old dream returned—not as a puzzle to solve, but as guidance to follow. The laundromat wasn't just about cleaning clothes; it was about cleansing the sentences we wear on our bodies.

I had been created to be an agent of possibility in a world that often feels like neverending chaos. To wash garments and sheets, yes, but also to cleanse words, thoughts, interactions, and relationships, so that dignity could return and stay.

Expression is the most powerful skill we have when we steward it with awareness. As a speech-language pathologist, I help restore communication, speech, cognition and swallowing. But my patients didn't improve just because I was kind or credentialed. They recovered because, in a world of suffering, I spoke life where others had declared an ending. As I honed this gift of language as medicine, I saw the difference clean words can make: peace returns, accountability becomes possible, the nervous system unclenches, choices change, and relationships heal. Clean words don't just describe reality; they create it.

Today, my work continues that promise. I help individuals and teams remember their voices and use them with intention. With individuals, I uncover communication patterns that have been quietly sabotaging their days, and together, we replace them with truer ones, practiced until they hold up under pressure. With couples, I weave tenderness into boundaries so that neither person has to disappear to keep love intact. With leaders and teams, I build cultures where honesty feels safe and dignity is non-negotiable. I teach caregivers to ask clearer questions so that the people they serve can say yes without betraying themselves.

If you've made it this far, you can hear the rhythm of my life, tested in fire, steadied in faith, and refined through language. The dragon still stomps somewhere beyond, wearing the masks of fear and accusation, but it no longer controls the street. The laundromat lives inside me now, bright and steady.

Gratitude keeps me grounded. I thank God for the breath that powers each sentence, for the memory that returns when it's needed and for the courage to remain present when a difficult story rises to the surface. My work is not about being spectacular; it's about consistency, a daily commitment to make language a place where people can heal. It's a willingness to keep folding what life hands me until the stack holds.

If parts of your life feel stubbornly stained, I know the way to the machines. If teamwork is scattered, I know how to rewire synergy without losing the heart. If your relationship needs a boundary that doesn't break love, I can help you find the words that hold both.

Bring me your basket. We'll start with one sheet: the phrase you repeat that quietly drains your power. We'll wash it, rinse it in truth, starch it with courage, and fold it into your daily language. Then we'll tackle the next one, and the next, until your words can carry your life again.

Language is medicine, if we choose to use it as medicine. When we do, chaos steps back, the aura brightens, and what we carry out into the world is clean enough to share.

If something inside you knows it's time to clean the language, reach out and simply write "laundromat." Tell me what's in your basket; one pattern, one conversation, one sentence that won't let you go, and we'll begin there, together.

ABOUT THE AUTHOR
HADASSAH ROSE, M.S.ED, SLP

Hadassah Rose, M.S.Ed, SLP, is a powerhouse speaker, workshop leader, and author who is redefining how we approach communication, healing, and human connection. With over 25 years of experience as a speech-language pathologist treating individuals with neuro-cognitive communication disorders, she developed *Language Decoding and Realignment,* a trauma-informed method that transforms destructive language patterns into resilience, clarity, and empowerment. She is also the author of *The Communication Lab – 50 Self-Reflective Experiments to Transform Your Communication in Everyday Situations.*

Clients describe Hadassah as deeply professional yet remarkably relatable. Leaders and executives praise her for creating safe spaces where authenticity and growth come together. Her intuitive approach helps professionals break toxic patterns, strengthen leadership presence, and build healthier relationships across teams and organizations.

Through her workshops, writing, and private sessions, Hadassah teaches that language is medicine, that the way we communicate shapes who we are, the networks we influence, and the transformations we create, one conversation at a time.

Connect at: https://stan.store/HadassahRose

7
_____

THE POWER OF COMPASSION AND PERSEVERANCE

THE JOURNEY OF DEVOTIONAL PRESENCE

BY INTHIRANI ARUL

*W*e all carry an inner calling. It's ours to notice, to respect, and to express it with purpose.

I was born in Malaysia into a Tamil family of Southern Indian descent. When I was three, my parents moved us to Canada, hoping to build a more stable life. My father worked for the railways, devoted to providing us security and support.

My mother's life was shaped by constant health struggles; diabetes, blindness, and mental illness. As her eyesight faded, her mental health declined too. By the time I was nine, I had stepped into the role of caregiver. As the eldest daughter, with my father away at work, I learned quickly how to manage medical emergencies and daily responsibilities. I cooked meals, kept the house running, made sure my mother ate on time, ensured her safety, and handled her medications including giving insulin injections.

School brought its own challenges. Anxiety weighed heavily on me, and learning felt like climbing uphill without rest. Doctors eventually discovered I had a vision impairment from birth, which made it even harder to grasp lessons or retain information. I even failed my first year of school. But I refused to quit. Each time I fell, I stood back up. In those early years, I discovered that perseverance would become my greatest strength.

I have always loved learning, and that passion made me a lifelong student. I finished high school, went to college, and completed many courses. My education kept going into adulthood through mentorship and guidance from world-class teachers. For all of this I am deeply grateful.

Loss and inner awareness

My mother lost her long battle with her health in 2003. A year later, in 2004, I faced another heartbreaking loss when my husband, our son's father, died in a tragic motor vehicle accident. In the middle of that grief, I became deeply aware of a yearning for a life of deeper meaning, something larger than I could yet imagine.

A clear sense of purpose, an inner knowing that I was here for something greater. My devotion to the Creator deepened, and I set out on a journey of self-discovery, growth, and greater awareness. Having received many blessings throughout my life, I felt deeply called to give back.

I started seeking out leaders who were creating real, positive change on the planet. With each meeting I sensed a spiritual connection to certain people, and I was drawn to that connection. That search led me to Mahendra Kumar Trivedi, known as Guruji, an enlightened and miraculous being, with the highest form of consciousness on this planet. I first saw him speak while watching an international summit, and his presence moved me deeply.

When I learned that Guruji was coming to British Columbia, I knew I had to see him in person. Together with my son and sister, I received a blessing from him, and in that moment, I knew I was standing in the presence of the Divine. It was a life-altering experience, one that forever shifted the course of my journey.

Through his discourses, I came to see how truly blessed and fortunate I was—to be invited to listen, to deepen my understanding, and to experience the joy of being in his presence, as well as in the presence of his wife, Master Dahryn Trivedi, and CEO, Master Alice Branton.

I know my life purpose is one of growth and the continuous elevation of consciousness. I am forever grateful to my beloved Guruji for blessing me with the opportunity to participate in three science experiments. These were, based on the mouse model study, where my abilities were measured, validated, and documented in peer-reviewed scientific journals. To be clear, I did not participate in any human-related studies.

By Divine grace, I was led to Guruji, and his blessings have transformed my life in ways I could never have imagined. I once lived with poor immunity, severe social anxiety, and a stutter that made communication a constant struggle. Today, my health and well-being have improved profoundly. I live with a calm mind, a peaceful heart, and an abundance of love that flows into every part of my life.

Through his guidance and blessings, I have awakened to a deeper awareness of my divine gift of empathy, and the responsibility to use it in service of others.

In 2018, while my father was in the Intensive Care Unit, I reached out to Guruji to share what was happening. The care I received in that moment was a gift beyond words. With gentle reassurance, he said, "Don't worry. I will take care, and I will bless you and your father."

When my father was passing, I felt a warm, loving presence that stayed with me even after he had left this world. In my grief, I called Guruji, not only to share the news, but to express my gratitude for the strength and comfort I had received through his blessings. With great compassion, he reminded me, "As human beings, we all have emotions. Our parents are the conduit that brings us into this world. They play a role in our life, and we play a role in theirs."

Those words reshaped how I experienced loss. Instead of only seeing the pain of his passing, I was able to honor the sacredness of our bond, the role he played in my life and the role I was able to play in his. It gave me a deeper understanding of love, presence, and the way our lives are woven together with purpose.

My life has evolved in many ways, yet one thread has remained constant.

Since early childhood, caregiving has been part of every chapter of my life. It began with caring for my mother, and by the age of sixteen I was volunteering in the long-term care wards at Vancouver General Hospital, where I spent more than five years serving elderly patients. For over thirty-five years since, I have dedicated my life to supporting adults with special needs, offering not only quality care but also empowering them to live with joy, purpose, and love.

I serve with patience, perseverance, and an open heart. I create environments where people feel safe to express themselves and encouraged to explore new experiences. Through activities such as baking, art, pottery, crafts, and guided learning, I help them discover their own capacity to make empowered choices and build confidence in using their voices. I take the time to truly know each person, their strengths and abilities, and I gently guide them toward action when needed. I love finding ways to inspire them to pursue their goals. I celebrate their progress, no matter how small, because every step forward deserves to be acknowledged.

When I am with those I serve, time disappears. I am fully present with them. My deepest intention is that they feel joy, that they laugh, that they feel heard, supported, and reminded of their abilities and potential. Whether someone is learning a new task for the first time or practicing the steps for the hundredth time, I meet each moment with love and steady determination. This is where my true fulfillment lies; giving love freely, from the heart.

The Power Within

My gifts of compassion, perseverance, patience, and a devotional presence allow me to hold space for others with unwavering love, calmness, and trust in their potential. I see people not only for who they are but also for who they can become. I recognize the abilities within each person and seek ways to strengthen them. I support others by understanding their strengths and challenges, their unique abilities, and their ways of communicating, always listening without judgment. I am not here to fix anyone, but to be fully present, consistent, and loving.

I feel the energy of others, and I carry the ability to bring calm into any situation. I observe, I process, I pause, and only then do I respond. This calmness is not only mine to carry but also mine to share, creating a space where others can find peace and clarity. When I speak, I feel honored to be heard. Yet I also know that silence itself is a powerful gift, the gift of listening without interruption, allowing others the freedom to fully express themselves.

The power within me has been shaped by many influences across my life. From an early age, loyalty to my family taught me devotion and responsibility. Prayer instilled strength, faith, and resilience. Mentors offered wisdom and guidance that continue to shape my path today. And kindness, whether shown in small gestures or great sacrifices, has always touched me deeply, often moving me to tears of joy.

These influences form the foundation of who I am and how I serve. Loyalty reminds me to stay committed. Prayer keeps me connected to divine guidance. Mentorship fuels my growth so that I may pour into others. And kindness is the thread I seek to weave through every interaction. These are the gifts I carry forward and the values I strive to embody as I walk beside others in their journeys of healing, growth, and purpose.

This inner power helps me remain grounded in love, face challenges with steady steps, and trust that every experience is shaping my growth and guiding me toward my destiny. Over time, I have learned to trust the still voice within, the voice sustained by my deep connection I have with the Divine. Perseverance strengthens me to keep showing up, even when the path is hard and the results are slow to appear.

Because of this, I am able to bring calm, compassion, and gentle encouragement into every situation. By listening deeply and holding space, both physically and emotionally. I create an environment where others feel safe, supported, and empowered. With devotion and determination, I give my time, energy, and presence fully.

Impact on others

When I bring my calmness, I often see visible shifts in others. Their faces soften, their eyes and mouths brighten into smiles, and even their posture changes. They stand or sit taller; their shoulders no longer slumped. It feels like watching energy itself transform, confidence rises, excitement grows, and productivity flows more freely.

Those I work with often experience emotional healing, personal growth, and a renewed sense of self-worth. They begin to trust themselves and the path ahead. They feel uplifted, supported, and encouraged, not only by my presence but also by the steady care and consistency I bring. My perseverance shows them that obstacles can be overcome and that goals, however distant, are within reach.

I have witnessed people grow in confidence, calmness, and trust. Many became more vocal, more willing to explore new experiences. Their quality of life expanded as they engaged socially and developed essential daily skills, cooking, cleaning, laundry, reading, writing, and caring for their homes and themselves. They discovered new avenues of creativity through baking, pottery, painting, and crafts. They began looking forward to community events, performances, and opportunities to share or gift their creations with others. Above all, they gained a stronger sense of independence and purpose.

One individual, for example, once lashed out physically at anyone nearby. Through consistent care and patient support, she transformed. Now when she needs help, she often asks for me personally. Rarely does she strike out, and if she does, she quickly catches herself and apologizes. More often, her instinct is to reach for a hug. Witnessing such transformation reaffirms for me the quiet power of compassion, consistency, and care.

Three individuals who became my teachers.

1. The Gentleman with Cerebral Palsy and Nonverbal Communication

He communicated "yes" by clicking his teeth and "no" by sticking out his tongue, sometimes vocalizing a soft "ya" or "no." To help him express more, I would slowly move through consonants and vowels, giving him the chance to form words. It required patience, attentiveness, and trust. Over time, his true voice began to emerge. He taught me that presence creates possibility.

2. A young man and the E-tran Frame

Another young man also lived with cerebral palsy and used both an E-tran frame and a Bliss board. Though wheelchair-bound, he had memorized more than 250 words. The E-tran, a clear board with numbered sections, allowed him to form up to a three-number combination by directing his gaze. I would then reference the Bliss board to identify the corresponding word, for example, 14 might mean "water," 20 might mean "food." He guided me with his eyes, and also turned his head left for "no," right for "yes," and would tilt his head down when unsure. His smile let me know when I understood correctly.

Six months into my job, I received an evaluation suggesting that I needed to "communicate more." That feedback became a turning point. I enrolled in courses, including Dale Carnegie's Public Speaking and Human Relations. During one session, I invited Rick to join me on stage. Together, we demonstrated how he communicated with the E-tran and Bliss board. Afterward, people lined up to meet him, and Rick was radiant with pride. He taught me that advocacy and visibility can transform the way the world listens.

3. The Elegant Lady Who Struggled to Trust

She was an intriguing older woman who found it hard to trust. She adored elegant clothes, jewelry, and beautiful shoes. Words were few, and at times her uncertainty or fear would erupt in screams. Over time, our relationship grew stronger. She valued routine, and honoring those routines brought her peace.

As her vision declined, a van would bring her to a program where she painted pottery and cards, the one place she still wanted to go. On difficult days, she sometimes refused to leave the van. But the moment she heard my voice; she would step out. She taught me that reliability, respect, and tenderness can dissolve fear.

Lessons Learned

Together, these teachers deepened my patience, strengthened my acceptance without judgment, and gave me the courage to advocate. They grew my confidence, sharpened my teamwork with families and professionals, physiotherapists, dietitians, doctors, nurses, and social workers, and taught me how to care through change, including the grief of losing a resident. Through them, I gained wisdom that continues to guide me on my own journey.

Disability vs. abilities — we all have abilities.

Working closely with people of diverse abilities has taught me that the word ability lives within the word disability. Some face physical limitations, while others navigate cognitive or emotional challenges. Yet every person carries gifts, preferences, a unique way of communicating, and a longing to be understood. Our role is to meet people where they are, be patient with the pace of learning, even when it requires repetition, and create environments where they can rise to their next level. When we slow down and truly listen, ability reveals itself. This is the essence of inclusivity.

Our communities should reflect this truth. We must recognize all abilities, acknowledging both strengths and weaknesses, and remember that we can all learn from one another. In doing so, we enrich not only our own lives but the lives of everyone we touch.

Why I Am So Passionate

I have lived both the pain and the purpose.

I know what it feels like to carry invisible burdens, to feel unseen, and to walk through the isolating valley of grief. I know the weight of responsibility and the exhaustion it brings, yet I have also learned the strength that comes from enduring, from standing firm even when the load feels too heavy.

I understand what it feels like to struggle with anxiety, low self-esteem, and the lingering effects of trauma. At an early age, I found my mother unconscious at home and had to call 911. I cared for her through years of health challenges while also facing difficulties in my own education. Later, my husband suffered a tragic death, and I lost my father as well. When my husband passed, I was left with a fully functional restaurant, a business I had never managed. Eventually, it was sold, only for the new owner to fail in fulfilling their commitments, leaving a difficult financial situation behind.

Family dynamics have also shaped where I am today. I have learned to let go of many things, some beyond my control and others no longer serving me.

Through it all, I have come to know the profound power of compassionate perseverance: showing up again and again, no matter how difficult the road. That perseverance has carried me through every season of life, and now it is what I offer to others.

I have experienced the magic of empathy, the healing that comes when someone truly gets you without needing explanation.

This work has transformed me on many levels. It has deepened my patience, strengthened my confidence, and taught me to communicate with clarity and compassion. Working with people with special needs has shown me multiple ways to connect and has revealed the beauty of unconditional acceptance. I have discovered that every person has an authentic way of expressing themselves, and when we listen with care, connection is always possible.

This path gave me a profound sense of purpose. It reminded me that every person matters and that each life is a gift. Living with social anxiety for many years, I found healing through the acceptance I received from the elderly and from the individuals I supported, they never judged me. Their trust helped me find my voice.

Professionally, I learned to provide quality care and advocate for those who are nonverbal. I developed skills in cooking and food preparation, feeding and supporting individuals with complex medical needs, including g-tubes, ileostomies, and colostomies, and assisting people with cerebral palsy who had little or no mobility with bathing and transferring. I organized celebrations, trained new staff, and became the go-to person on my team because of my experience. I learned to respond to medical emergencies, navigate staff shortages, manage challenging dynamics, and, importantly, set healthy boundaries for myself. This work widened and deepened my heart.

I have come to understand that everything in life is a foundation for our greater purpose, a purpose bigger than the life we see now. Patience is essential; everything unfolds in divine time, not our own.

For now, I continue to grow and increase my level of consciousness, so that I can have a greater impact on those around me and give back for all the blessings I have received. I believe our gifts are always meant to be shared.

Compassion softens pain, empathy bridges hearts, and perseverance creates safety, not just for others, but for ourselves as well.

From a time when I could barely speak, struggled with a stutter, and lived with anxiety, I can now speak from my heart, with calmness, truth, and presence.

I serve from a place of devotion to the Creator.

Women of Global Change

As an extension of my work, I became involved with an organization that aligns beautifully with my values and the way I live my life.

The Women of Global Change (WGC) is an international organization that empowers women leaders to create lasting, positive change in their communities and around the world. Founded by Dr. Dame Shellie Hunt, WGC brings together conscious, purpose-driven entrepreneurs, professionals, philanthropists, and change-makers who are committed to meaningful impact—locally and globally.

What They Do

1. Global Humanitarian Projects: Hands-on service such as refurbishing classrooms, building or supporting schools, and delivering supplies to underserved communities in places like Jamaica, Mexico, and the United States.

2. Leadership Development: Training and networking that grow conscious leadership, including public speaking, business strategy, social impact, and collaboration, all rooted in heart-centered service.

3. Empowerment Through Collaboration: Global chapters and retreats where women share their visions, support one another's missions, and co-create solutions that uplift humanity.

4. Recognition and Advocacy: Amplifying members' work through awards, media visibility, and speaking opportunities.

Core Beliefs

1. Service is a path to leadership.

2. Change begins within and radiates outward.

3. When women come together with purpose, they can shift communities, nations, and generations.

Vision

Every human being deserves access to clean water, food, health care, education, and income training - beyond race, creed, religion, or circumstance. WGC engages individuals to expand global engagement, business, and social impact. Those who serve, succeed.

Mission

A network of business leaders and entrepreneurs collaborating in global business, camaraderie, and service, creating outcomes together that none of us could create alone. Members participate in educational platforms and humanitarian projects for themselves, their communities, and the world.

My Involvement

I am honored to be part of this community of heart-led leaders committed to conscious action. With WGC, I have participated in international service projects, including refurbishing schools in the Yucatán and Jamaica. Being on the ground, bringing light and hope to children and communities, reaffirmed my life purpose: love in action transforms lives.

Through WGC, I have grown as a leader, deepened my global contribution, and celebrated the strength of compassion, empathy, and perseverance. Together, we are turning vision into action and service into legacy.

Coming Home to Love

As I reflect on my life, the caregiving, the challenges, the losses, the perseverance, the devotion, I realize my journey was never just about surviving. It was about remembering. Remembering who I truly am. Remembering every act of compassion, every choice to persevere, every time I showed up with love and care, every lesson along the way, and the devotion I committed to. No matter how small, how quiet, or seemingly insignificant, all those moments carry infinite power.

Every act of love, every choice to show up, every quiet moment of devotion has brought me closer to my truth.

We each carry something beautiful within us. For me, it has always been this, the power of compassion and perseverance expressed through presence and love. It is not loud, yet it speaks. It is not forceful, yet it transforms.

I remember doing Warrior Training for a week in the wilderness, with limited communications, and three-minute showers. That experience was profoundly transformative. I learned so much about myself, and it gave me the strength to follow my calling.

If you are reading this, wondering what your own power is, know this: your power already lives within you. Your light, your strength, your capacity to love, your resilience, your ability to keep going, they are already there.

You do not need to search outside yourself. Listen inward. Seek within. Trust your path. Let your life speak.

Always remember: the most extraordinary impact comes from the simplest acts of love, offered with empathy, anchored in compassion, repeated with patience, and carried through with perseverance.

That is the power within.

ABOUT THE AUTHOR
INTHIRANI ARUL

Inthirani Arul is a 4x best-selling author, a highly awarded Dale Carnegie–trained speaker, and the Vancouver Chapter President of theWomen of Global Change. She is known for guiding individuals to lead with their heart and harness their authentic power. With over 35 years of experience as a caregiver and advocate, her calling began at just nine years old while caring for her blind, diabetic mother, a journey that sparked her lifelong mission to inspire and empower others to face life's challenges with grace, pivot quickly in adversity, and embody the change they wish to see in the world.

From a shy, reserved child who faced daunting challenges including a speech impediment and vision impairment, Inthirani's journey has been one of resilience and transformation. These experiences not only shaped her character but also ignited her passion for helping others rise above their struggles and reach their fullest potential.

Through her books and speaking engagements, she shares a message of hope, strength, and the power of living authentically. What fulfills her most is the heartfelt feedback from those whose lives have been touched, uplifted and inspired by her work.

Beyond her professional endeavors, Inthirani is a lifelong learner, always seeking knowledge and wisdom. This commitment to growth and understanding lies at the heart of everything she does.

Connect with Inthirani:

🌐 www.inthirani.com
📘 facebook.com/inspire88
🌍 www.womenofglobalchange.com

8

HOW I FOUND ME

BY KATE KAPLAN

*M*y promise to myself in my early twenties was simple: I would do everything I wanted to do until I turned thirty. After that, I'd fall into line. And to my readers, that's exactly what I did. I took on a variety of jobs in advertising and retail, owned an exercise studio, earned a graduate degree, and traveled, meeting some wonderful people along the way. I had so many passions and so little time to give them all.

Then came thirty. Then forty. Before I knew it, at forty-two, I was living in Chicago with my husband, having just adopted twin girls, twins I had prayed for since I was eleven, holding my grandmother's and Mother's Novena prayer books in my hands for thirty-one years. Talk about faith and prayer!

My story begins on a summer day in Iowa, hot and humid, as it always is. But July 3rd, 2023, stood out, offering everything the perfect summer day should: warm, sunny, with a light, comforting breeze.

My day was designed for the public pool, a chair and book in hand. Can you relate to that feeling of being so ready for a moment of pure solitude, just for yourself? I took my last dip of the day, surrounded by the busy little ones, jumping in and sliding down the slide without a care in the world. It was pure pleasure for them—and for me too, at that moment.

But little did I know, feeling like a million dollars and warmed by the sun, an unimaginable moment was waiting just around the corner. Settle in now, turn off your cellphones, and acknowledge the work you've done in putting yourself first to read about a divorced, single mother's struggle with the unknowns of mental illness. I know I am not alone.

Bedtime came after a joyous day in our new home. We were just one week in. From atop the hill, I sat by the kitchen window, looking down the street where all the kiddos played. All within two years of each other. Our home was two-story with a fenced-in yard for our dogs. Wonderful light streamed in from every direction, thanks to all of its windows, one of the major pluses for me. And, of course, the gorgeous view of the sky in the morning, noon, and night, radiating from our backyard. It was my getaway, my place to take a breath and dream.

The girls ran through the house, from one big room to another, laughing and giggling, calling out, "Mom, put that there!" Our three cozy bedrooms were special, with each of my daughters finding a place for their stuffed animals and photos of friends and family.

Yes, all of their photo frames were of my kid's creations. As you read my story, I ask you to keep in mind a few thoughts that have haunted me over these twenty-plus years.

One: How do you push through the tornado of paralyzing fear that you think you're hiding from others, questioning when this will ever end?

Two: Where are the friends I desperately needed but pushed away, because they couldn't understand the challenges I was facing? They saw me becoming a loner, someone shut off, short-tempered, and they saw their children's behaviors mixing with mine.

Three: How does one reinvent themselves after more than twenty years of being so ensconced in debilitating, frenetic behaviors, and deeply stressful daily routines?

Yes, I am speaking of my daughter's early onset schizophrenia, diagnosed when she was just four years old. The chaos, the haunting screams, her sibling turning inward without emotional support or security from me, her mother, exhausted beyond my wildest dreams.

It is my desire to speak to all the caregivers out there, and I hope I'm doing that. I desire to speak with the people who care for an unwell or disabled parent, child, elder, spouse, or loved one with mental illness or other challenges. I want to reach out to all of you, and there are so many of you. Around fifty-three million Americans are caregivers, and approximately twenty-one percent of the adult population provides unpaid care to a loved one. That's nearly a quarter of the adult population in this country, and about sixty-one percent of that group are women. One in four of you is caring for a child under the age of eighteen, which could include those with special needs, mental illness, or developmental or intellectual disabilities. You're providing that care for an average of four to five years, or even longer.

Over time, you begin to feel resentful towards that person. Resentful that you've given every ounce of yourself, every granule of your life, to them. And then, just like that, guilt sets in. Guilt because you feel like you're not doing enough. Guilt because you dare to feel resentment. Guilt because you want out. Guilt because you want a night to yourself, just one night to read a book, go to the movies, or simply take care of yourself, if only for one single moment.

My darling twin girls were born after thirty-one years of prayer. You might ask yourself, "Really? Why?" Honestly, I don't know. All I can say is that I needed something to believe in, something besides God. And in that need, I found faith in prayer with purpose. It was then that God's plan for me began to unfold, though I didn't realize it at the time. Looking back, I know that many of the struggles I faced were teaching moments from God, preparing me for my children. I relied heavily on gut instinct, and though I was grateful for it, I still felt utterly lost.

Let me take you back to that unimaginable moment I spoke of earlier, one that would change everything. Here's a wild story that perfectly captures the unpredictability of my journey with my daughter's schizophrenia. God love her, she had put a warrant out for my arrest a year before.

The day I was swimming at the pool, hair wet, dressed in my swim-suit and skirt, heading home, I noticed police cars pulling out of a parking lot behind me. I thought to myself, I'll just merge right to let them pass. To my surprise, three squad cars boxed me in on a main street. They pulled me from my car, slapped handcuffs on me, and whisked me off to jail.

As we pulled up to the barbed-wire fence, I suddenly realized I had no rights. I was a sixty-nine-year-old woman, alone, scared, and with no way to contact a single person in that moment. Before I put on my jail uniform, I asked the attendant, as I stuffed my wet swim-suit and skirt into a plastic bag, if she could leave the bag unsealed so it wouldn't mildew. Now, that's one of those moments I now look back on with a bit of humor.

The small cell, with its metal door and narrow window, housed me and six other women. The only other fixture was a metal toilet, with a spout attached to the back of it, meant for drinking water but also draining into the same place we were all supposed to relieve ourselves. It was horrific.

My daughter's manic state had caused this chaotic and traumatizing ordeal. False statements about me came faster than I could even keep track of. Four days later, when I was finally released, I hadn't eaten or drunk anything, and I had kept every emotion bottled up inside me. Fortunately, a friend came to pick me up. But not even a mile down the road, I had them pull over. I needed the air. I needed to scream. I had to let everything out that I had been holding inside.

Not long after, I stood before a judge, tears in my eyes, hearing him tell me that the charges had been dropped. That moment stung, lingering for months after. My resilience, along with that of many others, has driven my passion for helping people navigate the often-overwhelming world of mental illness and caregiving.

Caring for my daughter was not only challenging but also isolating, and when engulfed in situations with no clear answers, I often felt completely overwhelmed. Caregivers need to know that they are not alone and that there is hope and support out there.

My story is one of resilience, compassion, and unwavering dedication. I've worked not only to change the lives of my own family but to reach countless others in need.

One important thing to know about me is that I like to live in what I call the "bliss lane." But what does that mean? Imagine being in the kitchen, following a recipe. You need the right ingredients and steps to make a delicious meal. Similarly, to create a happy and fulfilling life, we need certain things and actions to guide us along the way.

When I'm cooking, I like to add a little corn, some tomatoes, or whatever else catches my eye. It's a lot like life, right? We plan our days, trying to create moments that lead to a satisfying end. I've spent twenty-five years facing some tough challenges. We've slept on floors in outpatient areas, been kicked out of doctors' offices, and found ourselves surrounded by police in the E.R. But you know what? The next day always comes. And I've learned that I have to make sure there's a plan for it, whether it's for school, appointments, insurance, nutrition, or medications. The plan might not always go as expected, but that's the recipe of life. Now, am I a cook? Oh, absolutely! I love to cook and entertain.

During COVID, I even built a twelve-by-five-foot picnic table so my friends and family could all gather together. I asked each person to design their own chair to bring, just for fun. It's always a blast, adding a personal flair to our gatherings. There's never a dull moment. I have a quick story. One day, I was outside admiring a tree when my neighbor, who's much shorter than my five-foot-nine frame, shouted from across the street, "Kate, it's just a freaking tree!"

But to me, it was a moment of renewal, something we all need to find. Ever since I was a little girl, I would climb and sit at the tops of trees with my dog tethered at the bottom, looking at the clouds and watching the world below me. That was my moment of renewal. My bliss lane. It's a feeling we all need to experience, and it's what I want to help you find. Find your own recipe for living in the bliss lane.

The gift of friends, whether you have many or just a few, is being able to share both your wins and your challenges, without fear of judgment. Take a moment and think about it, do you have this kind of friend? Are you the one who always shares your struggles, feeling like you've spent all your time talking, without ever asking how they are? Or maybe you're the opposite, always the listener, always trying to please others?

Consider the richness of true connection, the kind where you're heard and valued, and where you can both listen and be listened to. These moments not only bring warmth but build lasting trust and acceptance.

Each day, we should prioritize taking care of ourselves because, for caregivers, true freedom comes from caring for ourselves first.

In our journey together, I want to dive deeper into some important things we all need to think about. First, let's talk about something we all probably strive for but often struggle with: getting in sync with ourselves. It's about finding that internal harmony, where our thoughts, desires, and actions align.

This begins with being present in the moment. It means reading the situation as it is, asking ourselves meaningful questions, and genuinely listening to our inner voice. You know, life gets busy, and it's so easy to get caught up in the whirlwind of daily tasks. But pausing, even for a short while to tune in to ourselves can make all the difference.

Here's the challenge many of us face: we often stand in our own way. We have these dreams and ambitions, yet self-doubt, fear, and even long–formed habits hold us back. It feels like driving with one foot on the gas and the other on the brake. What does this cause? We get stuck. Meaning, we are stuck in a cycle of wanting to move forward, but we don't quite let ourselves.

So, what's the way forward? It begins with hearing and picturing your dreams clearly. We need to value the wealth of our own experiences and accomplishments. Think about everything you've achieved so far, whether in caregiving or outside caregiving. No matter how big or small, those moments are your building blocks.

When you pause to recognize and value your own journey, the road ahead becomes clearer. You start to see not only what's possible but also what's within reach.

So, take a moment right now. Close your eyes if it helps, and ask yourself, "What do I truly want?" Listen to that inner voice and answer honestly, without judgment. You can write it down or simply let it speak to you. Picture your dream vividly, as if it is already happening. Feel the excitement and fulfillment it brings.

This exercise isn't just daydreaming. It's a powerful way to align your actions with your desires. Getting in sync with yourself means giving yourself permission to pursue those dreams. It's about stepping aside and letting your true self take the lead. When you do this, you create a path forward that feels natural and authentic; *because it is!*

After both of my daughters moved out of the house, I worked hard to find a community of caregivers. For over twenty-five years, I had placed men and women from the Philippines in people's homes as caregivers. Along with more than twenty years of caregiving for my daughter's illness, I hungered for a community of like-minded people to grow with.

For five solid years, that community supported and guided my growth. I understood that I needed this support to move beyond the frenetic chaos of my daughter's schizophrenia. Within that group, we gained momentum even when a day went wrong and we couldn't catch a break, we've all been there.

An example from my life was dealing with a problem I had repeated over and over to what felt like blank walls, hoping for a solid answer, only to receive yet another piece of bland, unhelpful advice. Frustrating, right? It felt like I was speaking a language no one understood.

Regaining my confidence started with acknowledging that my feelings and experiences were valid. My daughter and I lived these moments in full, even when others only see a part of them. We deserved to be heard and understood. Imagine the release of pressure when a cap finally pops off, that's what validation feels like. It's liberating.

For me, rebuilding confidence after years of navigating the medical system began with moments of vulnerability. It could be sharing with a trusted friend who truly understands, experiencing a breakthrough through self-reflection, or simply admitting to myself that my struggles are real and deserve attention. Knowing that someone genuinely understands what you're going through changes everything.

Building a community of like-minded caregivers made a huge difference. I began to realize that my struggles did not define me and were not insurmountable. I created these moments by finding my voice and speaking my truth, even if it felt like no one was listening at first. I kept advocating for the support and answers we deserved, surrounding my daughter and myself with people who respected and valued our experiences, and most importantly, reminded us that we were not alone.

The key for me was remembering that these toxic times were temporary. Wherever my strength came from, it gave me the push to keep going, and eventually, my confidence followed.

The isolation I felt because of my daughter's illness wasn't about being physically alone. It was about the sadness, shame, and burnout that crept in when I felt most disconnected. I was confused, unfocused, and begging God for just one normal day. Sleep didn't come easily; exhaustion had hit me like a ton of bricks.

But here's the thing, the cost of isolation is high. Yet today, as a community of caregivers, we are not alone. We are in this together. It's important to remember that there is always a way through the darkness. Feeling sad, burnt out, or confused is okay.

Recognizing and honoring these emotions within myself was my first step toward overcoming them. People in this community gave me the courage to reach out, celebrate my small wins, and keep building from there.

The bottom line is this: our tomorrows need us. Every step we take today brings us closer to a better, more connected future. What I've come to appreciate, something I hadn't fully understood before, is the importance of taking time for myself. Whether we are married, single, or somewhere in between, it often feels impossible to prioritize ourselves because there is always something else demanding our attention.

But here's the truth: making time for yourself isn't a luxury, it's a necessity. It's about maintaining your well-being, staying grounded, and keeping your sanity intact. You might ask, "How do we do that?" The answer lies in carving out essential 'me time' in the midst of our busy lives. It requires discipline and focus.

Through my work with a wide variety of groups, families, and individuals, I've learned how creativity, focus, and discipline build a resilient mindset. That doesn't mean I never fell. What matters is that I got back up every single time. I developed solid plans, conducted regular self-assessments, and followed through with the support of a community we called our Caregiver's Corner. Together, we developed the resilience to face whatever life threw at us, because we shared, learned, and grew together.

Through this engagement, I gained insights that I've applied not only to my own life but also to the lives of my clients. I've taken bits and pieces, and even big lessons from everything. I've experienced, and my goal now is to make a difference for those of you who are struggling.

Remember this: true freedom in caregiving comes only when you care for yourself first.

ABOUT THE AUTHOR
KATE KAPLAN

Kate Kaplan is a Des Moines, Iowa native, YouTube interviewer, and domestic/international recruiter for nurses. She is a 25-year business owner placing caregivers in private homes and has spent 29 years as an adoptive mother of twins navigating the challenges of mental illness and schizophrenia. Her experience has allowed her to impact lives across the country, working one-on-one, in groups, and as a speaker empowering parents, siblings, extended families, veterans' families, and elder caregivers supporting those living with mental illness and schizophrenia.

Respected for her ability to simplify complex topics into practical daily actions and habits, Kate shares her most powerful insights as a co-author of the book *"The Transformation Within: Finding Strength, Voice, and Vision."*

Connect with Kate: kkaplancaregivers@gmail.com

9

THE POWER OF ONE STEP

MY JOURNEY OF CREATING AN ABSOLUTE PLOT TWIST IN MY LIFE!

KATHERINE T. MOYER

*E*very great transformation begins with a single step. Not ten, not twenty—just one. That step might feel impossible, terrifying, or even reckless. But it's often the very thing that cracks open the door to freedom. My journey wasn't a straight line by any means. I definitely took the scenic route, full of potholes, pit stops, and plot twists. Maybe you can relate?

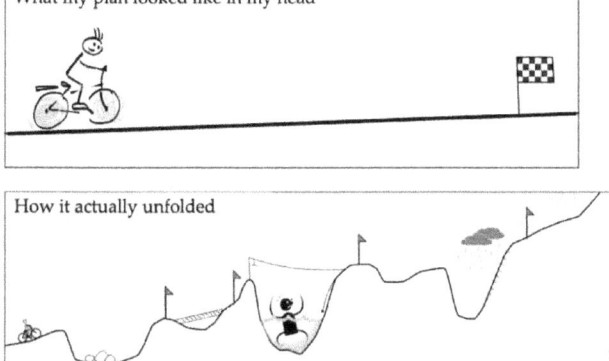

When my parents met, Dad was a Navy sailor in his twenties, already married with four kids. Mom, just nineteen, was caught up in a whirlwind romance that quickly swept them off to California. Mom got pregnant not long after, and they officially married when I was ten months old. By the time I turned two, they were divorced. Dad stayed in California, while Mom returned to Utah, where she had family support as a single mother.

By the time I was six, Mom was married to her second husband, and a baby sister arrived. By my thirteenth birthday, Mom had divorced her fourth husband, and Dad had divorced his third wife. Growing up, I shuffled back and forth between California and Utah every eighteen months. It gave me plenty of practice in adapting. New schools, new friends, new homes. "Constant Change" wasn't just a theme; it was my lifestyle.

What I missed in those early years was stability. The sense of belonging that allows you to breathe deeply and feel safe which was something I never quite had.

Those childhood experiences naturally transitioned into adult challenges. I moved from one address to another, held various jobs, faced a few bouts of homelessness, had a brief marriage that ended in divorce, and dealt with more than my share of drama and chaos. Something had to change.

It's funny how life works. Change rarely announces itself with trumpets. It often slips in quietly, disguised as **coincidence**.

One day, my astrology-loving hairdresser who always asked for the birth dates of my latest romantic interests, handed me a book. She gave me strict instructions: "Start at the preface. Don't skip around." At the time, I wasn't much of a reader, but once I began, a whole new world of understanding unfolded before me. That book marked a turning point in my journey. Until that moment, my future had seemed pretty predictable.

I couldn't put the book down, and at the end, the author listed eight pages of recommended reading. Captivated, I went on a treasure hunt and built an incredible library from her list. It wasn't easy, especially in the days before the internet and Amazon! But the deeper I dove, the more my mind opened to new ideas and perspectives.

Between jobs at the time, I spent six months immersing myself in learning and expanding my view of both myself and the world around me. The concepts were radically different from what I'd been taught in my childhood and family experiences. It was as if my "wisdom bucket" had been bone-dry for most of my life, and suddenly, it was overflowing. I couldn't get enough!

I grew up a "latchkey kid," raised by a single mother. We lived in low-income housing, bought groceries with food stamps to make it through the month, and my yearly wardrobe consisted of hand-me-downs from my older cousins. Watching my mom push through hardship after hardship planted something deep inside me. I wanted my life to be different. I wanted to rise above the struggles she had to carry alone.

Not long after, I landed the highest-paying job I'd ever had. On the surface, it felt like a breakthrough. But working in a family-owned business as the only outsider came with its own battles. I often found myself trapped in the crossfire of their family conflicts spilling over into the office. With all the drama, I asked myself, *"what am I really doing here?"* I asked the Universe, *"If this isn't where I'm meant to be, please, just give me a sign."*

They say, **be careful what you ask for**. Within a month, I was laid off and collecting unemployment. They also say when one door closes, another one opens. So, what if this could be my chance to start over, somewhere completely new? Why not? This could be the chance I really needed to break free and start a whole new life.

Just as I was beginning to seriously think about relocating, all hell broke loose! My family and life drama dialed up to full blast. It left me questioning whether this was a wise decision or a terrible mistake? Was the timing right, or completely wrong, or just some kind of test around my commitment.

Ultimately, I decided it was an opportunity to commit to myself and my journey. I knew if I stayed where I was, the outcome would be more of the same. After all those books and gaining a whole new perspective … Now that I know something different it's important that I **do something different**. Otherwise, I'm **choosing to stay where I am**. I wasn't sure what was going to happen, and I was willing to take the adventure of figuring it all out.

My final decision was destination: Dallas, Texas. I'd never been there before and didn't know a single person living there. This would be a **pivotal STEP** in my journey. I faxed out résumés, scheduled an in-person interview, booked a flight, and reserved a hotel and rental car. Long story short, more opportunities unfolded. They lost my reservation and raised the price. Frustrated but determined, I moved to another motel where, by some stroke of grace, a kind desk clerk offered me the senior rate, even though I wasn't close to being one. It felt like a small win in the middle of uncertainty.

And then, the next day … wait for it … the company had already filled the position, the one I had flown all the way there to interview for!

What? That was unexpected. Was THIS a sign from the Universe, or just another chance to go "all in" and put my survival and adapting skills to use?

I was disappointed, but I didn't let it stop me. I picked myself up and started searching for a place to stay while continuing the hunt for a job. I mean, what other option was there? Give up and go back to Utah? No way. I had already decided that was **no longer an option**. Feeling a little like Indiana Jones taking that **leap of faith** into the unknown. I kept moving forward, **one step at a time!**

I'm sure it's no surprise that more hurdles followed.

I found a room for rent with a nice elderly lady. Yes! One task down. Packed up from my motel room, went back to her place, and while I was gathering my things to move in, she rented the room to a traveling businessman. What? Shocked, I had no choice but to keep moving forward. So, back to the motel I went. Thankfully, they let me slip right back into the same room and even kept my senior discount. Sweet! Small blessings.

A few days later, after visiting several more places, I came across another room, this time with a nurse who worked ten days on and ten days off. She had two little poodles who needed care when she was gone. The arrangement came with two bedrooms, one with a sofa and TV, and my own bathroom. It was perfect. I was ecstatic to get settled in. The next day, my family friend, who had volunteered to drive my car to Texas, suddenly developed tennis elbow and had to cancel. With no other option, I booked a flight back to Utah.

Twelve long hours and four connecting flights later, I made it. I packed up my things, filled my car with only the essentials, installed a CB radio for emergencies, back then, not everyone had a cell phone, and headed out for the thirteen-hundred-mile road trip back to Dallas.

What an adventure that drive turned out to be. White knuckling through a blinding snowstorm, grateful for that CB radio, sandwiched in a convoy of truckers, keeping each other entertained along the way. During a quick dinner stop with my new trucker friends on the border of Texas, one driver leaned in and gave me the name of a local bar to stop by when I got to Dallas. "Tell the bartender I sent you," he said.

By the time I finally rolled into Dallas, thirty-two hours had passed without a wink of sleep, I finally made it. Whew, that was crazy!

After some much-needed sleep, I headed over to that local bar. I pulled up a seat and told the bartender how I'd heard about the place. What followed was an incredible welcome party. Drinks were poured on the house, and I was introduced to the locals, embraced as though I had belonged there all along.

While getting to know some of the regulars, one offered to introduce me to his manager at a large truck dealership the next morning for an interview. I gladly accepted—and was hired the very next day. The whole experience felt like fate.

My room rental soon came with additional responsibilities and expectations, and before long, conflicts started rising. Within just a couple of months, I found myself needing to look for a new place to live. Reflecting on my experiences, the best decision seemed to be getting my own apartment, though I wasn't sure how I could possibly afford it. Thankfully, my sales manager at the dealership stepped in and helped me find a nearby apartment. With a little credit card creativity, I managed to get settled into my new place, just a mile from work.

A few months later, that same sales manager shared a business idea. At that point in my life, I was feeling a little desperate to figure things out, so I was open to almost anything. I even wondered if this was **fate** giving me another chance. I agreed to the partnership, and before long we had filed the paperwork and created a new corporation. I left the dealership, bought all the computer equipment we needed, and even converted my small apartment into a space to meet with clients and run the business. My new business partner generously agreed to pay me a monthly salary until the company became profitable.

Well, that didn't turn out as smoothly as fantasized. The months that followed were filled with drama and stress I never saw coming. Keeping a long story short, eventually the obvious hit me. I had to cut my losses. By then, I was already down a staggering $17,000, and I knew if I didn't walk away, that number would only grow. It was a significant blow, but I had to believe, once again, **when one door closes, another door opens**. So, I went back to the drawing board for another pivot.

I had to remind myself; **I can't start my next chapter if I keep re-reading my last one.**

More drama with purposeful direction continued. Of course, it didn't feel like that at the time. Hindsight is typically where all the dots connect and everything becomes clearer.

With a brief and messy dating experience, I was connected with the owner of a temporary agency. After scoring high on several assessment tests, they placed me in a position as a technical support agent with an international retailer. Proving once again that **everything happens for a reason!**

Not coming from a technical background, I remember sitting in that two-week onboarding training and hearing the same warning again and again: *"If these standard terms are unfamiliar to you, you're probably in the wrong place."* Naturally, I'd never heard the terms before and would likely fail the test after training and be looking for another job opportunity. But hey, it's at least two weeks of pay to take care of a couple bills. As mom always said, every penny counts. So, **I showed up each day, paid close attention, absorbed what I could, and did my best.** Although I had used computers in previous positions, I didn't know anything about how they actually worked.

To my surprise, there was no final exam. Straight to a desk, taking incoming calls and being supervised while putting all the training to use. I was just happy to continue making a paycheck.

Seven months later, they offered me a permanent position. Whew, what a relief. Now I could start concentrating on my debt. Between relocating to Texas, struggling to find steady work, pouring money into a failed business venture, and living off credit cards, it was now up to $60,000! It felt like it would take the rest of my life, but I knew I had to start somewhere. I made a budget and kept taking one small step at a time towards a zero-balance goal, focusing on how much stress that would take off my shoulders.

I got too comfortable. I let my guard down, took my eye off the target, and those old limiting patterns began resurfacing. Soon, I found myself on a list of "problem employees," with the head of the department just waiting for the right moment to say, *"You're fired."*

Moving thirteen hundred miles away from my dysfunctional environment and starting a new life in Texas wasn't the magical fix I was hoping for. I noticed familiar drama and chaos showing up all over again, this time with different names and faces.

And there it was. The blinding yet painful flash of the obvious. There is only one common denominator here. **Everywhere I go, there I am.** And THAT is where changing ANYTHING begins.

It became clear, if I wanted something different, I needed to **become someone different**. And becoming someone different would require me **doing something different**. And **more different** than just changing my geographical location.

The journey to figuring out HOW came with another blinding flash of the obvious. **I was trying to outsource an inside job.** If I wanted true and lasting change, it had to come from within.

It was time to step it up.

Once again, recommitting and refocusing on becoming a better version of myself, the Universe rose up and met me there, leaving a powerful trail of breadcrumbs to follow with books, courses, and conferences. Although I was getting closer and closer to that zero-balance goal, the breadcrumbs felt like a necessary investment in the big picture of my journey. Essentially, I decided **I was worth it!** Albert Einstein's quote kept running through my mind: ***"We cannot solve our problems with the same thinking we used when we created them."***

In my seventh year of creating a new life in Texas, those breadcrumbs led me to something amazing that lit me up inside and had me running as fast as I could to learn more.

With **fate** and **nudges** in full swing, I took **another bold leap** with a weeklong vacation and a road trip to San Antonio to dive deeper into the biology of perception and the psychology of change. Holy crap (and yes, that's the censored version)!

When I returned to work on Monday morning, it felt like I'd done a quantum leap into a parallel universe. Everyone noticed something drastically different about me. Colleagues wanted to hear all about where I was and what I had been doing. Even the head of the department was curious. Evidently, I returned a version of myself I didn't even know was "in there!"

The next several months were all about committing to my own inner work. Every aspect of my life improved. My self-esteem, confidence, performance, communication, and relationships. Within six months, I went from being on the "short list" for termination to earning two major promotions! What a transformation.

The head of our department showed up at my desk on a Monday morning and dropped a bomb: we had twenty-five contractors in the conference room starting their second week of training, and the trainer had called in sick, so I needed to go up there and fill in.

"What?! 🐻 Why me?" Apparently, I was the only one who had a grasp of what they were learning 😳.

With no way out, I begrudgingly headed to the conference room.

There they were, twenty-five strangers staring at me, expecting me to teach them something. Without an outline of the training material. I started by asking a few questions to understand what they had actually learned so far and where they were. I was surprised after an entire week, they didn't know more. I did a quick pivot and went off the cuff, deciding to cover the "big picture" of how the network, hardware, and software all worked together.

Thankfully, the trainer was back at work Tuesday, and that was over!

Then came Wednesday. The big boss called me into her office. She said, "So, I hear you found your niche." I said, "What do you mean?" Her reply was: "Word is, the contractors learned more from you in one day than they did all last week!"

The Universe was at it again, providing me with an opportunity (although that isn't what it felt like in the moment) to discover my superpower. That turned into promotions as Technical Trainer, Technical Writer, Technical Manager, and ultimately, Trainer of Trainers.

As they say, hindsight is always 20/20. Yet another opportunity to understand even more deeply that **EVERYTHING is happening FOR ME, not TO ME.** The Universe is always conspiring to support me, even when it's unrecognizable in the moment!

Several months after that transformative trip to San Antonio, another blinding flash of the obvious hit me. **I have to share what I learned.** My whole life had changed in the most unexpected ways. Impressed with my personal shifts, even the supervisor and the head of the department decided to attend the same courses. I knew others really needed and wanted this kind of transformation in their own lives.

After successfully completing the requirements, I was certified and am one of only twenty-eight Worldwide Instructors, supporting those seeking real and lasting change on their own sacred journeys.

The most amazing adventures continued for eight years. I spent weekends offering workshops, loved my corporate career, and truly felt I was living my best life. It felt like I was exactly where I was meant to be.

Then came another hard decision.

In 2008, big changes began at my corporate job. People retired, departments merged, and the culture went through an unexpected shift. Co-workers fell ill, and some even transitioned. Showing up at the office just didn't feel like I was where I was supposed to be anymore.

My very first job had been at sixteen, and by thirty-one, I'd been fired from every job I ever held, always within months of starting. Now, I had been with my company for fifteen years. I earned five weeks of vacation, had a 401(k), an impressive salary, but the economy was crumbling. We were in a housing crisis, people were losing their homes, and tent cities were appearing everywhere. Walking away from everything I had built didn't feel like the smartest decision, or the right time.

I had reached my debt-free goal. And in July 2010, at forty-five years old, I retired from my corporate position. This was **another one of the hardest decisions I've ever made.** I felt like I had achieved ultimate success with my original decision to move to Dallas, and I had to trust that the Universe would rise up to support me again, as it always has. And support me it did!

Jumping ahead to my life today.

WOW, what an adventure! When I took that bold leap to San Antonio twenty-three years ago, I never could have imagined how amazing life would become. Not only did I retire from a rewarding career with a Fortune 150 company, but those courses I traveled to San Antonio for have become my life's passion.

After fifteen years of "software problem-solving," moving into teaching "mindware problem-solving" felt natural. Today, I travel internationally and love holding space for people to identify and transform what keeps them stuck in the reruns of old programming and conditioning.

I am so grateful for this journey and for the opportunity to offer hope, inspiration, and tools to brave souls from all backgrounds, to re-write the software of their minds and change the printout of their lives.

The gifts in my life are countless, including twenty-nine years with a husband who loves supporting other courageous souls learning this sacred work. Having the ability to maintain inner peace throughout the ongoing worldwide chaos and transitioning of many friends and family. Living with a deep knowing that **everything is happening for me, not to me, is the biggest gift of all.**

The filters, interpretations, and conditions of my early years contributed to layers of illusions, blocking me from peace, joy, love, and all things good in life. Having tools to support the recognition of my value, worth, and divinity as intrinsic, and knowing I have all the internal resources and capacity to create a joyful, purposeful life along the way has been **priceless.**

True, it's been messy at times, and I am eternally grateful for every single step on my path. Grateful that I listened to that deep inner calling. Grateful that I didn't let FEAR or my conscious mind take me out before giving myself a real chance. Grateful for how my path continues to reveal itself as I make my way. Grateful to all those who invite me to witness and participate in part of THEIR amazing journey!

During our human experience; we build layers of illusions that separate us from our truth. When the personal timing feels right, I believe everyone can benefit in using this cutting-edge, ancient wisdom. With so many paths available for change, don't cheat yourself! You deserve to step into the greatest version of the grandest vision you could possibly imagine.

It's never too late for change. You only need **a little courage, to take one empowering step that could change everything**. Your "future self" is cheering you on and waiting with open arms!

Time is the only thing you can't get back. If you feel stagnant or stuck and a desire to shake things up, level up, or take a quantum leap is stirring in your heart and soul, act now before your conscious mind takes you out. **Let's meet sooner rather than later!**

No matter what your story is, where you come from, what you look like, what you've been through… every single day, you are still writing the story of your life. The coming chapters could have a wild twist!

Kat is a client who started her plot twist and shares this small part of her journey:

After the very first session with Katherine, I showed up at my 12-Step meeting and felt like a square peg in a round hole. I just couldn't relate to any of it. I tried again the next day, but it was clear, I no longer belonged here. I was tapering off medications feeling anxiety, panic, depression, insomnia, and extreme body pain. Those symptoms faded away. After our second session, I resolved an eating disorder and an ongoing GI tract issue that involved a traumatic experience. The transformations were so natural it left me wondering "How could any of this ever have been a thing?!" Katherine's ability to balance solutions and the heart is one of her greatest gifts! Another gift is really being present and not shying away from the difficulties and challenges that clients bring for their sessions.

Ginger, another client shares:

I arrived at Katherine's proverbial doorstep with a lifetime of grief, loss, neglect, and trauma that stripped me of my authentic self and who I desired to be. Resistance held me hostage. Katherine didn't blink, judge or hesitate as she met me where I was, took me by the hand and together we embarked on the adventure of reconstructing my psyche. Eradicating limiting beliefs. Transforming decades old programming. I've won a new life lottery ticket. Now free from invisible shackles of torture, I speak to myself with kindness, understanding, compassion and love. I flow with ease from moment to moment. I face challenges, gliding gracefully in accepting them. No longer self-abandoning; I show up for myself and prioritize my needs. I openly share my heart a little more. I frequently find pockets of joy. I embrace my quirks. I witness my becoming and allow my radiance to lead with audacity!

So, what comes next?

Where are you right now in your journey? Is the impact of your perceptions brand new to you? Do you consider yourself well-versed in various therapies of change and transformation? Are you a professional who supports others with their healing and success? These simple, self-empowering processes complement all religions, belief systems, and modalities while **meeting you exactly where you are**!

If having empowering tools feels like the right next step in your journey, our workshops, both live online and in-person, offer an easy to learn, step-by-step "do-with" process. Rather than outsourcing the power to a practitioner, our processes honor that the power is in YOU. We'll partner with your inner wisdom to transform the beliefs necessary to reach your conscious goals and desires using built-in protocols that ensure every step is safe and appropriate along the way. Private one-on-one sessions are also available, whether long-distance or in-person.

ABOUT THE AUTHOR
KATHERINE T. MOYER

Katherine T. Moyer is an authentic, straight shooter most appreciated for her ability to help people see themselves and life in new ways. She often weaves humor into the serious work of self-realization and our deepest desire for purposeful living.

Drawing on her own messy life "aha" moments and a 15-year career as an IT trainer, technical manager, and problem solver, Katherine discovered her greatest passion in 2002. She now teaches internationally, holding sacred space for students and clients to clear the way for their own divine wisdom to appear and completely rewrite the next chapters of their lives. Those who have worked with Katherine often say, "If you want big changes in your life and are serious about making them happen, just buckle up and jump! Your life will change in amazing ways!"

Visit **www.EnhancedPotential.com** and let's start writing your wild twist!

Connect with *Katherine*:
https://linktr.ee/katherinemoyer

10

THROUGH THE CRACKS, LIGHT FOUND ME

BY NICOLETTE HALLADAY

For so long, I lived under the illusion that my worth depended on outward recognition. I thought strength meant holding everything together, no matter the cost. I believed having a voice meant staying compliant, not speaking truth, as if my value rested on how well I performed for others. And I convinced myself that vision meant stepping into a picture others painted for me, even when it didn't reflect the one within my own heart.

That illusion promised safety, belonging, and a kind of counterfeit currency. But betrayal, after betrayal, slowly peeled away the layers, revealing the truth to me.

That true strength comes from emotional honesty, true voice comes from speaking the truth, and true vision comes from trust. And just like a thread pulled through fabric, our stories are what reveal these treasures in us.

For me, this journey has meant writing my way into strength, voice, and vision. Writing became the space where I could embody what I was learning and share it with others. These are the three strands I want to explore with you here: strength, voice, and vision.

Finding Strength

After my divorce four years ago ending a twenty-year marriage, it felt as though every emotion I had ever pushed down came rushing to the surface. At first, it was mostly sobbing, almost everywhere I went and all the time. I cried in meetings, on calls with colleagues, while teaching in classrooms, and even during networking events. Sometimes the tears just flowed steadily; other times, they erupted in a storm that seemed impossible to contain. It was embarrassing at times, but it was real, I didn't fake it. My body refused to keep pretending everything was fine.

About six months after separating from my husband: my car was stolen. It felt like the universe was adding insult to injury, one more blow in a season that had already taken so much from me. Not long after, a few friends and I drove out to the desert, armed with a box of bottles and a couple of bats. We lined the bottles up against the rocks and smashed them to pieces, yelling until our throats were raw. Each shatter felt like releasing not just the car or the marriage, but years of frustration, exhaustion, and carrying burdens no one person should have to bear. The desert became my release.

But it wasn't only grief and anger that moved through me. For the first time in decades, I also felt free. Free from the invisible weight of managing a household, a marriage, and raising three children while working full-time. Free from constantly bending myself to fit someone else's expectations. There was hope rising in me too, the hope that I could build a new life, on my own terms.

Nature became my sanctuary. I would sit by the river, tears streaming down my face, and the water never once asked me to stop crying. The trees didn't try to fix me. The sky didn't look away soberly. They simply held me, exactly as I was. In that acceptance, I found the first sparks of my own strength. Writing.

Yes, writing. It became my refuge. Pouring my unfiltered experiences onto the page was liberating. My words weren't just a lifeline for me; they became a lifeline for others who carried their own silent griefs and hopes. The more people read what I wrote, the more they gathered around me. My honesty built connections. My vulnerability created a community. And that community, in turn, became the foundation for my publishing company.

Writing my way through the tumult attracted incredible authors who were eager to join me in sharing their own stories.

These experiences have taught me a very important yet simple truth: Strength is not found in holding it all together, but in expanding our capacity to feel it all; to feel the grief, rage, joy, freedom, and hope. Every emotion carries us closer to who we are.

Looking back, that season was my initiation into strength. My tears cracked me open, and through those cracks, light poured in. Shattering glass in the desert unleashed emotions that had been trapped for years. Sitting by the river taught me that my feelings weren't problems to fix, but truths to honor. And writing gave me the courage to share that truth with others, truth that became the foundation of my identity, business, my community, and my true calling.

Strength, I discovered, is not stoicism. It's not about never crying or pretending everything is going smoothly. True strength is the willingness to be undone; to rage and to rejoice, to grieve and to grow, and to trust that by feeling it all, we are being rewoven by something wiser than ourselves.

That was the gift of strength: the courage to stop filtering who I am. But long before I found this strength, I had already been nurturing something that would carry me through the challenging times, which was my voice.

Finding My Voice

Finding my voice meant letting go of the weight of others' expectations.

I had to let go of the need to be "nice" when "nice" was really just people-pleasing.

I had to stop dimming my light to make others feel comfortable.

I had to walk away from relationships that tried to shape me into someone I wasn't.

I had to let go of the desperate need for universal acceptance.

We can never find our true voice if we are still performing for others' approval.

I also had to let go of the belief that my spirituality was something to be ashamed of. For years, I silenced my connection to Spirit, as if it were something to hide. But eventually, I understood that my voice could not be separated from my soul. Our voice becomes sacred when it rises from our deepest truth.

About ten years ago, during this process of shedding layers, I received a download: *Write to Connect.*

I began writing openly about motherhood, about working a nine-to-five, about the messy, beautiful chaos of being a woman juggling it all. I wasn't writing to impress anyone. I was writing to connect.

One of those posts, which resonated deeply with many people, was about the moment I began to see myself again, after years of carrying the weight of motherhood and trauma. I wrote:

"I see with my mind's eye a beautiful radiant being waving at me. I lost total sight of her several years ago. I wasn't sure I'd ever get to see her again. That confident and hopeful young lady went missing after a surprise and stressful pregnancy and traumatic emergency cesarean to my third beautiful daughter, McKenzie Sue. I wasn't kind to my body after I had McKenzie and it didn't want to heal… All while trying to tend to the needs of my two older daughters who were in desperate need of a mother who was whole. Four year old McKenzie is thriving now… But my scars lingered. I pushed myself to work harder, love deeper, exercise intensively, and yet that piece of myself seemed gone. But now, I see her again. I feel that beautiful, strong, and put together lady in my presence again."

That post opened the floodgates of connection. Other women began sharing their stories of loss, resilience, and rediscovery. My honesty became an invitation for theirs.

The more I wrote, the more I realized my voice wasn't just for me, it was a bridge, opening up others' portals. People connected with my words, and opportunities started to flow. What began as vulnerable Facebook posts eventually led me to support others online as a virtual assistant. From there, it lead me into publishing, first supporting other publishers and, eventually, founding my own company.

Those early posts grew into chapters and books. I published a journal filled with prompts to help others discover their voice. Now, I'm writing something I never imagined a year ago: a spiritual fantasy that leads people through the sacred alchemy of loss and healing, reminding them that their greatest power has been within them all along.

When we start using our voice, it doesn't stay small. It multiplies. What begins as a whisper can grow into a body of work. What starts as a single post can ripple into a book, a business, a movement, and even a legacy.

But to find your voice, you must first connect to your vision, the spark that gives your voice direction and power.

Finding Vision

I was born with vision in my eyes. As a Pisces sun, a dreamer through and through, I've always seen possibilities woven into everything around me. Over the years, this gift has been both a blessing and a curse. Nothing weighs heavier on the heart than vision without belief.

I struggled with this for a long time. I could see visions in an instant, feel it pulsing through me, and see its potential stretching out before me. The energy of possibility would surge through my veins, and I'd get swept away by it.

And then I'd share it with those around me. Sometimes the people I loved could see it too. Sometimes they even lit up for a moment. But almost as quickly, doubt would creep in when they are faced with their own disappointments and fears would rise to the surface.

Believing felt too risky, too vulnerable. And when they lost their belief, I often lost mine as well. A vision without belief can collapse under its own weight.

There were times when the wobble was mine alone. I would remember my false starts, which were my photography business, reselling merchandise, multi-level marketing companies, and supporting my husband's side ventures. I was always reaching for something bigger, something beyond the mundane responsibilities of life, motherhood, and a demanding full-time job. But when those ventures fizzled, I would tell myself not to get carried away again, not to risk another heartbreak. That hesitation broke more visions than I can count.

But vision is resilient. It does not vanish, even when we abandon it. It stays quietly within, waiting for us if we might realize and grow into it.

One of my first experiences in truly leaning into self-belief was when I left my corporate job as a transaction coordinator for a business broker and took the leap to open my virtual assistant business. At that time, my six-year-old daughter was struggling with such severe anxiety that she would throw up every day before school. My boss showed no sympathy, and one day, something inside me roared: *You are more than this.*

I gave my notice without a plan. I had just a hundred dollars left in my bank account when, almost out of nowhere, two big retainer clients seemed to land in my lap, like a dream come true. Before I knew it, I was earning more than I ever had in corporate work and, more importantly, I had created the space to be fully present with my family while building the kind of business I'd always dreamed of.

That leap taught me something vital: vision isn't meant to be proven first, it's meant to be trusted. Our visions often start as a fragile spark; dreams, downloads, and whispers that feel too delicate to survive. But when we choose to believe, those sparks grow into the powerful current that carries us into the life we were always meant to live.

Over time, I've learned to approach my visions with greater care. I stopped scattering them too quickly and began sharing them only with people who could hold them gently. Mentorship and coaching provided safe spaces where my visions could be nurtured with grace, rather than met with skepticism. Most importantly, I learned to follow excitement without demanding certainty, to leap into the experience without clinging to a fixed outcome.

Sometimes, the true gift of a vision lies not in what it produces, but in who we become through its pursuit. The lessons learned, the people encountered, the skills gained, and the resilience built are treasures that no failed venture can take away.

Now, when I feel that spark, I'm more willing to leap, more willing to follow it's shimmer without letting the wobble of doubt undo me. Every vision is a teacher. Every pursuit is a stepping stone.

Vision resides within each of us. It doesn't need proof to be real. What it requires is trust, devotion, and the courage to keep showing up, long before others can see it too.

Vision. Strength. Voice.

These three threads have shaped my life, and they are woven into yours as well. I once believed that vision was about fitting into a mold others had set for me, but now I understand it is rooted in trust. I once believed that strength meant holding everything together or doing things all by yourself, but I've come to realize that true strength lies in emotional honesty. I once thought that voice was about compliance, but I've learned that words are born from truth.

For me, this has shown up most clearly through writing. Writing has become the way I display my strength, express my voice, and give form to my vision.

It is also why I now help others bring their stories to life. Every page, every chapter, every book begins with a single thread inside you, waiting to be remembered. When you follow that thread onto the page, you not only transform your own life, but you also create a bridge for others to step into theirs.

Your story matters. And when you share it, it multiplies.

If there is a story stirring inside you, don't wait for proof before you recognize that it matters. Trust that inner spark. Put pen to paper. Begin. The world needs your vision, your strength, and your voice. Your story might just be the bridge someone else has been waiting to hear.

ABOUT THE AUTHOR
NICOLETTE HALLADAY

Nicolette Halladay is a storyteller, publisher, and a catalyst for transformation. As the visionary behind Inspired Hearts Publishing, she dedicates herself to helping heart-centered entrepreneurs and change-makers bring their stories to life. Through her work, she amplifies voices in a way that fosters deep connection and meaningful impact.

Since founding Inspired Hearts Publishing, Nicolette has had the honor of supporting over 100 authors in sharing their stories, whether through multi-author collaborations or solo books. She has produced and published six anthologies and guided the creation of more than 50 published works. For Nicolette, each project is a testament to her belief that stories are not just words on a page, they are powerful bridges that heal, connect, and open the door to endless possibilities.

Nicolette's own journey from virtual assistant to publisher was born from personal upheaval. This transformation led to profound self-discovery and a deep mission: to help others share their truth unapologetically. A proud Colorado native and mother of three daughters, Nicolette thrives on deep, meaningful conversations, wild adventures, and meaningful connection that weaves through every story she helps bring into the world.

Have you ever thought about writing a book?

Start here: https://offer.inspiredhearts.co/home-page

11

BORN TO HEAL

REMEMBERING I WAS NOT BROKEN

BY PEGGY SUE CONNER

A Complete Journey of Transformation

Part One: The Awakening

"You weren't born to fit in. You were born to remember. To heal. To lead."

The First Act of Defiant Love

*A*t just nine years old, I committed my first act of radical healing.

I rescued my dying rooster, whose name was Chicken Legs. He lay there lifeless, barely hanging on, his tiny body trembling, his eye bulging out of his head. Scared and unsure, I looked to my mother for advice, but she told me to throw him away. I couldn't. Something ancient inside me awakened.

Quietly, I snuck him into my bedroom, wrapped him in blankets, and held him close in the dark of my closet. I whispered to him and loved him back to life—not because anyone told me how, but because I remembered. Deep inside, I just knew what he needed: water and love.

Looking back now, I understand that what I did wasn't just instinct —it was energy healing. Pure, untaught, divine love flowing through me as if it had always been there, waiting to be remembered.

Chicken Legs didn't just survive; he thrived. He became my best friend, following me everywhere after that healing. Every afternoon, he would wait on the front porch for me to return from school, flapping his wings with excitement the moment he saw me. He was my companion, my mirror, my first patient.

I didn't know it then, but I was already practicing.

That first act of defiance was more than saving a small creature—it was a declaration to the universe: I would not ignore the truth of my own energy. I would follow it, even when the world told me to look away.

Touchpoint #1 – Feel Your Power

Pause for a moment. Close your eyes and place your hands over your chest. Feel your heartbeat. Imagine it sending warmth through your body, as if you were sending love to yourself the way I sent love to Chicken Legs. Notice the energy you carry—always there, even when no one acknowledges it.

Breaking the Cycle

As I grew older, I began to feel everything—deeply. Pain. Injustice. Silence. I could sense what others were hiding beneath their smiles. I could feel the stories people didn't want to tell, the pain they were desperate to hide. I was the kid who felt everything no one wanted to talk about. The kid who wanted so badly to help, but somehow always seemed to be in the way—too much, too emotional. It was easier for others to dismiss me than to understand me.

What I felt to be right, I was told was wrong. And what I felt to be wrong, I was told was right. My entire body rebelled against the logic of it all.

I often knew what to do, but that never made sense to the adults around me. "How could a child know anything about adult situations?" they would say. I was never taught how to handle that kind of sensitivity. And in a world that rewards numbing, I became a target for my own emotions. Not understanding them and being told I should be something other than what I was, left me confused, hurt, and eventually angry.

So, I turned inward.

I made myself my own study. Every sensation became a clue. Every emotional storm became an opportunity to ask: *Why?* I began talking to my body and listening—not judging. I stopped labeling my symptoms as flaws and started interpreting them as messages. I spoke to my body as if we were best friends, as if it were whispering secrets I needed to hear.

Chronic fatigue? That wasn't weakness; it was depletion from over-giving. Chest pain? That was unspoken grief. Anger? Well, that was the hurt and fear I had never allowed myself to acknowledge.

The answers didn't always come easy, and when they did, they weren't always comforting to handle. Some of the answers shook me deeply, stirring emotions I didn't even know were buried inside me. There were moments when the truth felt too heavy, and I found myself wrestling with the realization that many of the struggles I faced were ones I had unknowingly created for myself. I found myself unraveling patterns I hadn't realized I was creating uncon-sciously. Self-sabotage seemed like a daily ritual, and I couldn't always understand how or why.

Little by little, I began to map the terrain of my emotions, tracing the hidden corners of my own heart. And in that process, I discov-ered something unexpected—the very pain I had spent years running from was actually the most powerful guide I could ever have.

Touchpoint #2 – Map Your Emotions

Take a deep breath. Bring your awareness to one recurring emotion that has challenged you. Where do you feel it in your body? What color, shape, or temperature does it carry? Simply notice it—without judgment. This is your emotional body speaking, your first step in decoding your internal map.

The Body Speaks Truth

I came to understand that healing isn't about fixing something broken—it's about remembering what was buried beneath the shame, blame, and guilt. For years, I carried others' opinions of me as if they were facts. I lived in false truths, and my body knew it.

I stopped seeing my body as something that needed to be managed and began honoring it as the sacred messenger it had always been. Every headache, every tight muscle, every low mood—all carried whispers from my subconscious mind. The migraines, especially, were the ones that spoke the loudest. They showed up every time I swallowed my anger, every time I forced myself into silence. I was so young when they first began that I remember calling them "green headaches," because I couldn't even pronounce the word migraine.

What began as simple curiosity slowly became a way of life—a personal methodology for healing.

Through breathwork, visualization, self-hypnosis, and deep subconscious inquiry, I started creating my own inner healing practices. I learned to call my power back, to rewrite the story I had once believed about myself. And each time I chose to feel instead of numb, each time I listened instead of silenced myself, I became stronger.

Not harder, just wiser, softer, and more whole.

Mini-Visualization – Rewriting Your Story

Close your eyes. Imagine a version of yourself weighed down by old stories, fears, or limiting beliefs. See yourself slowly lifting them off, one by one. With each weight removed, replace it with warmth, clarity, and energy flowing from your core. Notice how your posture changes. Feel your nervous system recalibrating, like tuning an instrument to perfect pitch.

From Fire to Framework

I came to realize that my nervous system was the secret map to my healing. My emotions were not enemies to silence, but intelligent messengers guiding me toward what needed care. My body, honest and unfiltered, would never lie to me. Every sensation, every emotional surge, was a conversation between my emotional, mental, and physical selves. When they aligned, this trinity became my power—and my true freedom.

The more I learned to regulate my emotions, the more I began to heal. And the more I healed, the more I remembered that I was never broken—that I was always designed to feel deeply, to sense, to know. My intuition wasn't a flaw or a weakness; it was the quiet blueprint of my becoming.

Touchpoint #3 – Integrate Your Trinity

Place one hand over your heart and one hand over your stomach. Take three slow, intentional breaths. Feel your emotional, physical, and mental bodies aligning. Sense the coherence between them. This is your trinity activating. This is your power. This is your freedom.

In quiet moments, after migraines softened and storms settled, I began to hear something new—not fear, not criticism, but my own knowing. Every surge of anxiety, every collapse into exhaustion, every spark of joy—they were signals, invitations from my emotional and physical selves. Energy doesn't lie. You can smile through pain, push through exhaustion, numb the ache. Yet beneath it all, your energetic field tells the truth. Align with it, and the nervous system recalibrates, the body reorganizes, and the soul remembers its power.

I have seen miraculous things happen—chronic pain vanish, autoimmune symptoms dissolve, mental fog lift, and emotional patterns that once felt impossible break open with grace. Not through magic. Not through theory. But through presence. Through conscious work. Through deep emotional honesty and energetic alignment.

One man, consumed by self-criticism, began sleeping deeply, waking with focus and motivation, stepping into a clarity and purpose he had never known. A woman who had worn glasses for forty years no longer needs them. She told me, "I had no idea my emotions were tied to my vision. This has changed the way I look at myself, the way I talk to myself, the way I take care of myself. Learning to see me—and what I truly need—cleared up my vision and helped me see everything else so much clearer."

These transformations are not coincidences—they are quantum shifts.

The Power Within

This work doesn't come from books or countless teaching sessions. It comes from my bones. From my own healing journey. And it has been my greatest privilege to guide others through that same portal of remembrance.

But my journey took an unexpected turn—one that would test everything I had learned and push me into territory I never anticipated. It would reveal the true depth of the healing power we all carry within us, even when we don't yet understand it ourselves.

Part Two: The Test of Faith

The Call I Couldn't Ignore

It all began with a phone call overheard by chance—a call that would set in motion a journey both mysterious and transformative. My youngest son's father was speaking with his mother about his uncle, Sherm, who lay in a California hospital, dying of congestive heart failure and kept alive only by life support. The family, bracing for the inevitable, was preparing to say their last goodbyes, as Sherm's living will meant the machines would soon be turned off.

In that moment, a powerful, inexplicable feeling washed over me. It was more than a thought; it was a calling—so strong that ignoring it felt like betraying something greater than myself. The voice I had known since childhood, my Jiminy Cricket, was speaking with undeniable clarity: *Go to California. Go to Sacramento. Visit this man and his wife.*

I didn't know them at all. I had never been to Sacramento. The obstacles were many: a winter storm watch around Lake Tahoe, logistical challenges, and skepticism from my son's family. Yet, I couldn't shake the certainty that I was meant to make this journey, and that the reasons would reveal themselves in time.

So, with my two-year-old in tow, I left Idaho and headed west.

Following the Signs

Throughout the three-day trip, I remained deeply present, refusing to let my thoughts drift to past regrets or future worries. My mantra became *"no expectations, follow the signs from the universe."* Whenever things seemed not to go my way—like when I struggled to find a hotel because the credit card didn't match my ID—I reminded myself to trust the process.

In a twist of fate, the hotel that finally accepted the card was just six blocks from the hospital, far closer than the others I'd tried. By now, it was clear: I was being divinely guided.

Arriving at the hospital, I felt both nervous and determined. My son's family remained skeptical, except for Sherm's wife, who had kept vigil at his bedside for weeks. She was exhausted, heartbroken, but open. Something in her recognized that I was there for a reason.

Unsure of what to do, I called my hypnotherapist, who advised me to place my hands on Sherm's head and trust that I would know what to do next. With faith in the universal guidance I'd felt all along, I entered his room.

Becoming the Instrument

I introduced myself to Sherm, though he couldn't respond. Then I began speaking directly to his mind. I told him that his brain still worked, that he could tell his body to start functioning again, and that he didn't have to be afraid of dying in the hospital. I placed my hands on his head, and something shifted.

The energy in the room transformed. It felt as if I was merely a tool —the hammer—while the universe itself was rebuilding the house that was Sherm. I wasn't doing the healing; I was simply the conduit for something far greater than myself. The same energy that flowed through me when I held Chicken Legs as a child was now flowing through me again, stronger and clearer than ever before.

I spoke to every cell in his body. I reminded him of his power. I held space for his healing with every ounce of love and faith I possessed.

Miraculously, within a week, Sherm walked out of that hospital. He lived another decade with his family, surrounded by love, before passing away years later on his own terms.

The experience left me awestruck, grateful, and forever changed.

The Shadow of Misunderstanding

Yet not everyone saw it as a miracle.

While Sherm and his wife were deeply appreciative, others in the family, especially those with strong religious beliefs, became fearful and suspicious. They accused me of witchcraft. They questioned my intentions. They couldn't understand what had happened, and what we don't understand, we often fear.

The pain of their rejection and misunderstanding was so great that I didn't speak of the experience for fifteen years. Another family member urged me to keep it secret, and I agreed, tucking this profound moment away where no one could judge it—or me.

But silence has a cost. By hiding this truth, I was denying not only my own journey but also the possibility that my story could help others remember their own innate healing abilities.

As time passed and I grew into my career, I realized the importance of sharing my story. The voice that had guided me since childhood whispered once again: *It's time. Tell them. They need to remember too.*

The Frequency of Healing

Through this journey with Uncle Sherm, I discovered that true healing exists as a frequency—a state of being we can embody through emotional self-awareness and mindfulness. This isn't magic or witchcraft. It's the natural state of consciousness available to all of us when we clear our hearts and minds of limiting beliefs and trust in the guidance of the universe.

I learned that by taking full responsibility for my perceptions; by remaining present and open, I could tap into a higher vibrational state. This is the frequency I strive to maintain, and the reason I now share my story openly: to inspire others to remember their own innate healing abilities and to co-create a world of higher consciousness together.

Touchpoint #4 – Quantum Awareness

Take a slow, deep breath. Imagine yourself as more than your body. See yourself as a wave of energy, flowing, expanding, connecting with everything around you. Notice how this awareness shifts something inside you. You are not limited. You are quantum. You are possibility.

We are all natural-born healers; it's in our DNA. The journey is about remembering, trusting, and embodying that truth—moment by moment, day by day.

Part Three: The Tools of Transformation

"You do not need to be fixed. You need to be felt. Seen. Heard. Held—by you."

After years of turning inward, unraveling my own emotional pain, confronting generational trauma, and stepping through experiences like the one with Uncle Sherm, I began to realize something profound: the very power that healed me—and flowed through me —could be shared and taught.

Not in the way most people expect, not through quick fixes or surface-level strategies, but through a deeper reconnection with self. True healing comes when you stop outsourcing your power and start listening to the ancient intelligence already residing within your body.

These aren't just techniques. They are sacred practices. Lived truths. They weren't born in theory but forged in the trenches of emotional alchemy. They form the foundation of my private practice, my courses, and every class, workshop, and webinar I teach.

In this section, I share the core tools that transformed my life and are now transforming the lives of those I guide. These practices lead people into radical self-awareness, emotional liberation, and the delicate art of nervous system regulation.

Because real healing isn't about changing who you are—it's about remembering who you were before the pain surfaced.

1. Emotional Mapping: From Triggers to Truth

Emotions are messengers, not problems. In my work, I guide people to become emotional cartographers, helping them map the vast and often tangled landscape of feeling. Instead of labeling emotions as good or bad, we honor them as sacred messages from the subconscious.

When a trigger arises, we don't push it away or suppress it. We lean in, with curiosity and compassion. We observe it by asking ourselves:

- What is being activated right now?
- Where does this emotion arise from my body?
- Which memory or belief is it connected to?

This emotional mapping gives voice to what's been trapped for years —sometimes for generations. It shows us how to stop reacting and start responding. It's how we begin to heal—not just the mind, but the inner child, the lineage, and the soul.

2. Nervous System Recalibration

You cannot heal if your body doesn't feel safe. This is a proven fact.

I have seen many people move through life in survival mode. They are constantly on alert, caught in patterns of fight, flight, freeze, or fawn—often without even realizing it.

My approach to healing centers on daily nervous system regulation practices—simple, intentional rituals that bring the body back into a state of safety and coherence. These practices include:

- Grounding rituals, like standing barefoot on the earth, walking in nature, or immersing in cold water
- Bioenergetic breathwork
- Somatic release exercises
- Gentle pauses for the nervous system, using sound, tapping, or conscious breathing

When I work with clients and students, I guide them to build rituals that honor their unique bodies. Healing is never one-size-fits-all. Safety must be customized.

When I work with clients on nervous system recalibration and subconscious reprogramming, we're not just addressing surface-level patterns. We're diving into the quantum nature of consciousness itself. Anxiety, limiting beliefs, or emotional reactivity aren't just thoughts—they exist where your awareness meets the field that connects all things.

3. Subconscious Reprogramming & Hypnosis

The subconscious mind is like fertile soil—it will grow whatever seeds we plant. But too often, we inherit seeds we never chose. Many of us were raised with fear-based programming, patterns of trauma, or disempowering beliefs that quietly hold us back.

Through guided hypnosis and subconscious reprogramming, I help people:

- Rewire limiting beliefs
- Release inherited trauma
- Imprint new, empowering emotional experiences
- Move from survival mode into a place of authentic self-worth

These sessions often unlock memories we've buried, heal long-standing inner child wounds, and spark real lasting changes in behavior. Many clients say they feel lighter, freer, more fully themselves than they have in years.

4. Intuitive Healing & Inner Guidance Activation

Everyone has intuitive abilities. The problem is, most of us were taught to ignore or even distrust them.

In my programs, I guide clients to reconnect with that inner guidance system that's always been there, quietly waiting. We explore and awaken abilities like:

- **Clairsentience** – the body as a tuning fork
- **Heart coherence** – feeling the truth instead of overthinking it
- **Intuitive decision-making** – learning to choose from a place of inner alignment

I teach clients to truly speak to their bodies, to ask it questions, and to pause and wait for its wisdom. And over time, we have experienced beautiful things: their intuition becomes their compass, replacing fear-based choices with decisions that feel right to their souls.

5. Emotional Alchemy & Energy Codes

Emotions are energy in motion. And when we learn how to move that energy, how to truly alchemize it, everything changes.

I guide people in emotional alchemy through a blend of Energy Codes work, visualization, and intentional energy practices. This isn't about avoiding or suppressing what you feel. It's about letting emotions complete their natural cycle, so they no longer hijack your nervous system or control your life.

We breathe through shame until it softens. We release anger from the body. We transform grief into sacred insight, finding meaning in even the heaviest losses.

Through this process, clients discover something extraordinary: they begin to feel powerful within their own emotional landscape. They stop fearing what they feel.

6. Integration Through Ritual & Reflection

Healing isn't something that only happens in a session. The real work begins in what you do with it afterward.

I guide my clients and students with integration rituals that help them anchor and embody the work:

- Mirror work
- Journaling prompts
- Sacred movement
- Nighttime intention setting
- Emotional check-ins, to listen to what their body truly feels

Healing isn't a project. It isn't just a response to a crisis. It's a lifestyle.

This Is My Work Now

I no longer try to prove myself. Now, I live my proof.

Every time I step into a webinar, host a course, or sit with someone one-on-one, I don't come with a script. I teach from a place of experience. I bring my scars, my lessons, and the weight of everything I've lived through. I teach from a place that has been tested by fire—not from theories. I walk with people straight into the fire—and out the other side.

I've seen what life's heavy circumstances can do. I've watched them crush entire families, tearing apart what was barely holding on in the first place. I've seen children lost because their parents were already lost, too. And the harder we try to fix what we don't even understand, the heavier the burden becomes. It's a painful cycle, running through generations, destroying one family after another. And it needs to stop.

I affirm this because I know what's possible. I've witnessed women let go of years of trauma they once thought they'd carry forever. I've watched men cry for the first time in decades. I've seen people heal —transforming their health, their relationships, and their entire energetic field—because they finally learned how to communicate with their inner being.

This is why I no longer have to prove anything. The lives transformed around me are proof enough.

This is what I do now. I hold the light until others find their own.

Now, I teach people how to:

- Feel what was once too heavy to feel.
- Speak the words that once felt impossible to say.
- Reclaim what was once abandoned.
- Love what they were once taught to reject.

Not because they need saving. But because they're finally ready to remember who they are.

Your Invitation to Remember

This is your invitation to step into your true nature—not as a limited biological machine, but as a quantum being capable of co-creating reality with the universe itself. Your awakening is more than personal growth; it is a return to your natural state of consciousness, a conversation with life itself. Every time you align with your energy, every time you reclaim your emotional sovereignty, you participate in a cosmic dialogue that has been unfolding for billions of years.

You don't have to follow someone else's path. You don't have to heal the way they said you would. You only need to trust that the power within you is real. And that's enough.

This chapter of my story isn't about overcoming. It's about reclaiming.

This is the power of radical responsibility. Of emotional sovereignty. Of walking yourself home.

And it's why I do everything I do now.

Because I know healing is possible. Because I've lived it. Because I was born to heal—and so were you.

If you are one of them—ready to feel, to reclaim, to rise—then know this: everything you need is already within you. The power was never somewhere else. It has always lived quietly inside you.

And when that moment comes, I would be deeply honored to walk that path with you.

A Practice to Begin

Before you fall asleep tonight, place your hand over your heart and say softly to yourself:

"I trust my body. I honor my emotions. I reclaim my energy. I am whole. I am capable. I am free. I am happy to be me."

Take a deep breath. Receive. Remember.

The healer you've been searching for has been with you all along, quietly waiting for you to acknowledge.

Listen. Feel. Remember. Trust your body. Honor your emotions. Reclaim your energy. Never doubt the intelligence flowing through you, even right now. Everything else—clarity, joy, purpose, true freedom—naturally and viscerally follows.

Your awakening is real. Your healing is real. The world needs the expression of your aligned, conscious, quantum self.

You are whole. You are capable. You are free.

ABOUT THE AUTHOR
PEGGY SUE CONNER

Peggy Sue Conner is a transformational guide, subconscious reprogramming practitioner, and emotional alchemist who helps people heal at the root by decoding the language of the body. Her work is anchored in subconscious integration, nervous system regulation, self-hypnosis, energy healing, emotional mapping, and intuitive guidance. What began as her own journey through childhood trauma, chronic pain, and suppressed emotion evolved into a life-long study of how the body stores—**and releases**—unresolved experiences.

Peggy Sue now teaches clients how to move from survival to sovereignty by working with the subconscious mind, regulating the nervous system, and treating triggers as sacred messengers. Through private sessions, workshops, and group programs, she guides others to reclaim emotional ownership, dissolve inherited patterns, and access the body's innate blueprint for self-healing.

Her core methods include:

- Subconscious Reprogramming & Hypnosis
- Nervous System Recalibration
- Emotional Mapping & Alchemy
- Energy Work & Intuitive Healing
- Embodied Inner Guidance Activation

Connect with Peggy Sue:
Facebook: facebook.com/peggysueconner
TikTok: @PeggySue4you
YouTube: @PeggySue4you

12

EMBRACE YOUR AWESOMENESS THROUGH CELEBRATING WINS

BY PIA BECKER

"Confidence isn't something you find. It's something you remember, each time you choose to see your brilliance and celebrate your truth."

---

*D*ear Dreamer and Wanderer, welcome to my world of Dream and Wanderland!

I'm Pia, the girl who once set out to explore the world and returned as a woman who had grown, stumbled, risen again, and discovered that she alone is responsible for her own path. Today, I know who I am, at least most of the time. And on the days I forget, I lean on the tools I've learned to guide me back to myself. One of those tools is what I'd love to share with you today, my fellow Dreamer and Wanderer.

But before we dive in, let me introduce myself a little more. My life feels like it's split into two chapters: everything before my first solo trip in 2014, and everything that came after.

Since childhood, I dreamed of traveling the world. I would sit with my dolls, imagining us boarding boats and sailing from one island to the next, discovering new places together. For a while, I let those dreams fade. Life distracted me. But one day, in a Geography class, we began discussing the continents and their unique wonders. And just like that, the dream that had once lit me up as a child came rushing back, this time, with a pull I could no longer ignore.

Fast forward 15 years, and I eventually made my dream come true. It took time to realize that the only person who could make it happen was me. Me. I.

One day I had enough of getting "no" from friends when I invited them to join me. I blamed them for the fact that I couldn't see the world. How could I travel when no one would come with me?

Truthbomb number one: you are the one who lives your life, not your friends or anyone else. I learned that the hard way. If I wanted to travel, then I should just do it, whether alone or with company. So I did.

That decision is what I write about again and again in my celebration journal. Keep reading to find out what I put in it.

Confidence does not arrive in one grand moment. I had to learn that too. From the outside it looks natural, but from the inside it comes and goes. Most of the time I just do me, and I am fine.

But when I am alone, those voices creep in. The ones that tell me I am not good enough, that I do not know enough, that I have not done anything to be proud of. The voice says I am in my thirties and still not where I want to be. The fact that for a long time I did not even know where I wanted to be does not trouble that voice at all. It made me feel low. Sometimes it made me feel depressed. Worst of all, it made me believe I had failed myself, my dreams, and my life.

Do you recognize this voice too? Sometimes it's loud, sometimes soft, sometimes even aggressive. It doesn't matter how it shows up, most of us know it in one form or another. Call it your Inner Critic, your Gremlin Voice, Ms. Never Enough, or even the Perfection Police, it wears many masks.

Too often, this critic tries to steal your spotlight, downplaying your wins and dimming your shine. But here's the truth: you don't have to listen. This chapter is an invitation to shift the narrative, to silence that voice of doubt by witnessing your own growth and embracing the powerful truth, you are already more than enough.

Every win, every step forward, every brave decision deserves to be seen. Let celebration become your fuel, and watch your confidence grow from the inside out.

Confidence doesn't come in one grand moment. It builds quietly, each time you choose to see yourself clearly, acknowledge how far you've come, and celebrate what you once thought was impossible.

Silencing Your Inner Critic and Unleashing Your Potential

The moment I realized my inner critic was sitting in the driver's seat, deciding how I lived, how I saw myself, and how I defined my worth, was a literal lightbulb moment.

I was unboxing the hard copies of my first book collaboration. The book had just made it to the New York Times bestseller list, and we authors celebrated with an online party. Soon after, the package arrived. I tore it open, heart racing, and there it was. I held the book in my hands, flipped through the pages, saw my face alongside my chapter. For a brief moment, I felt proud. Then I set it down, sat back on the sofa, and felt miserable about myself and my life.

Boom. What a reaction to one more dream come true, writing a book and becoming a bestselling author. Instead of joy, that voice returned, whispering that I hadn't achieved anything.

But then something clicked. Excuse me? I wrote a chapter in a bestselling book. I am a published author. I poured my heart into those pages. People bought it. People read it. What more do you need? I shouted back at that voice.

In that moment, I made a bold decision: I swore not to let that voice run my life. That's my job.

The best idea I had was to start a brand-new journal, my Celebration Journal. A place where I could write down every win, big or small, every success, every creation I had manifested, or would one day manifest. Proof that my inner critic was wrong.

That became my second truth bomb, the decision that changed my life. From that day on, I made it my mission to share this tool with as many people as possible to help them see their true selves, silence their inner critic, unlock their potential, and embrace their awesomeness.

Because, like me not too long ago, millions of people wake up each morning to the same uninvited companion: a voice that whispers, or sometimes screams, limitations, doubts, and criticisms before their feet even hit the floor. This inner critic is perhaps the most persistent and persuasive enemy of human potential, operating from the shadows of our consciousness with surgical precision. It knows exactly which buttons to push, which fears to amplify, and which dreams to diminish.

"You're not smart enough for that promotion."

"Everyone will laugh at your idea."

"You've failed before. What makes you think this time will be different?"

These aren't external voices. They're the internal soundtrack playing on repeat, shaping your decisions, limiting your actions, and keeping you trapped in a comfortable cage of mediocrity.

What most people don't realize is that this voice isn't telling the truth. It's telling a story, a story based on outdated information, past wounds, and fear-based assumptions. And more importantly, it's a story you have the power to rewrite.

The inner critic operates with such subtlety that many people don't even recognize its presence. It disguises itself as "being realistic," "staying humble," or "protecting yourself from disappointment." It presents itself as a voice of reason, a wise counselor keeping you grounded. In reality, it's the voice of fear, limitation, and self-sabotage, dressed up in the clothing of prudence.

This voice becomes so ingrained in our mental landscape that we often mistake it for our own authentic thoughts. We defend its harsh assessments as "just being honest with ourselves." We accept its limitations as facts, rather than recognizing them as learned patterns of thinking, patterns that can be unlearned, challenged, and transformed. I know because it happened to me. For the longest time, I lived with that voice without even noticing it, believing those stories about myself were true, and feeling miserable as a result.

Understanding the Inner Critic's Origins

Your inner critic didn't appear overnight. It builds slowly, shaped by experiences, messages, and beliefs. Recognizing where it comes from is the first step in loosening its grip.

Often, this voice begins outside of us: a critical parent, a harsh teacher, a competitive sibling, or cruel peers. Over time, those voices become internalized until they sound like our own. What started as someone else's judgment becomes our inner judge, jury, and executioner.

For me, it began in school. My German teacher never gave me fair grades on essays because I didn't share her opinion. She told me I was wrong again and again, silencing me for years. As an adult, I still catch myself second-guessing: if my thoughts weren't "right" back then, how could they be now? Even today, when someone contradicts me, I feel that old wound flare up, even though I know I am prepared and correct.

Here's the irony: the critic often begins as protection. As kids, we think, If I criticize myself first, maybe others won't. What starts as self-preservation eventually becomes the very thing holding us back.

The critic thrives on comparison, perfectionism, and worst-case thinking. One failed presentation turns into "I'm terrible at public speaking." One rejected proposal becomes "My ideas are worthless." One breakup can spark the thought, "I'm unlovable."

We live in a world that profits from insecurity: ads reminding us of what we lack, social media feeds showcasing curated lives, and definitions of success based on external metrics rather than inner fulfillment. Add our brain's natural negativity bias, the wiring that notices threat more than wins, and the critic has endless fuel.

And underneath it all? Fear. At its core, the critic is terrified of rejection and humiliation. I still remember how being called out by a teacher felt like death itself. That's how primal it can feel, as if survival depends on staying small.

Over time, the voice becomes so familiar that we stop questioning it. It creeps into thoughts and actions, even into the subconscious, until that whisper feels like your own truth.

The Hidden Cost of Internal Criticism

So, what happens when we let that voice run the show?

The cost goes far beyond discomfort. Chronic self-criticism literally rewires the brain for pessimism and self-doubt. It floods the nervous system with stress, clouding clarity and decision-making. To the body, there's no difference between being chased by a tiger and being attacked by your inner critic, both trigger the fight-or-flight response.

The critic also steals opportunities. I delayed traveling solo for three years because mine insisted, "You can't do it without friends." It took two more years before I launched my website, haunted by, "Who would care what I'm doing?" When I was invited into my first book collaboration, the critic nearly shouted me out of it. My body and mind went wild with doubt.

Even when we succeed, the critic swoops in to discount it. Publish a book? "You just got lucky." Travel the world while working full-time? "Anyone could have done that." Instead of celebrating wins, we downplay them, deflect compliments, and focus on what's missing.

It also strains relationships. Constant self-criticism makes us assume others judge us as harshly as we judge ourselves. We become defensive, blocking intimacy and collaboration. In professional settings, it silences us in meetings, keeps us from asking for promotions, and convinces us our ideas don't matter. The result? Careers and dreams are limited not by outside forces, but by inner lies we've mistaken for truth.

Celebrating Your Wins: The Art of Strategic Self-Appreciation

So, how do we break free from this cycle of criticism? By choosing to celebrate what is already true about us.

When I held my first book in my hands, I should have celebrated, but instead, I felt miserable. I found myself in a hole, thinking my entire life was a failure. Then the lightbulb went off. I realized that no matter what this voice is telling me, I must celebrate that moment as fully as I can.

As I mentioned earlier, I picked up a brand-new, beautiful journal on one of my travels and brought it home. I named it My Celebration Journal and began writing. I wrote down anything that came to mind, any win, any success, anything I had created in my life.

This book. My chapter. The fact that someone invited me to contribute. Living the dream of exploring the world. Every country I've visited so far. The apartment I live in. And more. I did it to show that inner voice just how wrong it was.

I made it a habit, at least once a week, ideally more often. Fridays became Celebration Friday. I even hosted a series of Celebration

Circles, where we collectively acknowledged and celebrated ourselves and each other.

Everything I've mentioned about the inner critic, its influence, its consequences, and its impact on self-perception, can be reversed through this simple but powerful practice.

You may ask, why acknowledgment and celebration, especially if you already practice gratitude?

Gratitude opens the door. Celebration invites you to step fully into your power.

At that time, I was already familiar with the concept of gratitude and had practiced it because some of my mentors recommended it. I tried it for a while, but it never truly resonated with me in a way that felt genuinely helpful. Being thankful for everything, whether I could influence it or not, like the sun rising and setting each day, felt, if I'm honest, almost like empty words.

Yes, gratitude helped me appreciate myself, my life, and the world around me. As a tool, it guided me toward mindfulness, helped me connect with my authentic inner voice, and even opened a channel to the divine. But for me, it felt passive, and therefore not as power-ful. In the end, the sun does what it wants, with or without me. I struggled to maintain a gratitude routine because of that.

Then I discovered that acknowledging and celebrating my creations is far more powerful. This practice focuses on the wins and successes I've actively created. It aligns with what I need to counter my inner critic and proves, in a tangible way, that there is no reason for her constant negativity.

Since I began celebrating my wins and creations, I think and feel more positively. I even feel proud of myself, a completely new expe-rience. My confidence has grown, and I no longer hesitate when someone asks me to contribute to a book. I know I have something valuable to share, and now I do it without second-guessing myself.

I literally silenced my inner critic; I proved her wrong. Today, it feels like she's sitting on my inner couch with a book in her hand, whispering in a relaxed way: "You can do that! No worries! If you need me, I'm here, but I believe in you."

The Acknowledge and Celebration Ritual

This is why I chose this topic for my chapter: I want as many people as possible to make peace with their inner critic. In the end, it only wants to keep us safe. By proving that we are safe, and capable, we can keep our inner critic in a calm, peaceful state. Over time, we can retire it from the driver's seat and take control of our own lives.

To do this, we need a practice, a ritual we can follow. Given the conditioning we experience growing up, the cultures we inhabit, and the ways the world operates, it's far too easy to fall back into old patterns of self-criticism instead of celebrating our achievements.

When starting out, I can tell you it isn't always easy to find something to celebrate. We're so conditioned that even the most remarkable achievements feel ordinary and unworthy of recognition. But the truth is the opposite: even the smallest win, every bit of progress, every action taken, every dollar in your bank account, or even a minus balance is worth celebrating. Why? Because you created it. And simply knowing you have the power to create at any time is reason enough to celebrate.

And here comes truth bomb number three: you're a creation machine! You cannot not create. You are creating all the time. And if you can create a minus in your bank account, you can also turn it into a plus. You have that power!

Plus, when you focus on your wins, you align yourself with the universe. And guess what? It's been waiting for you to appreciate the grandest creation of all: YOU.

You've probably heard the quote, "Where focus goes, energy flows." Imagine what happens when you focus on your achievements and successes.

You won't just silence your inner critic; you'll attract and draw even more of what you celebrate into your life.

We need to cultivate the habit of deliberately recognizing and celebrating our successes. This isn't arrogance or self-aggrandizement; it's about building an accurate, empowering relationship with your own abilities and achievements, and then using that power to shape the life you envision. And yes, the very act of envisioning your dream life is a superpower worthy of celebration.

So, what might this look like in practice? Create small but intentional rituals to acknowledge your wins, big and small. I love journaling because writing by hand activates the brain and body in a way that typing never does. You can also share your achievements with supportive friends or a trusted circle like my Celebration Circle, or pause for a quiet moment of acknowledgment. The form doesn't matter as much as the consistency.

Many of us are quick to celebrate others but hesitate to celebrate ourselves, believing it's boastful or unnecessary. That's just the inner critic trying to keep you small. In truth, self-celebration isn't about being better than anyone else; it's about honoring your own growth and progress.

Choose celebrations that feel authentic to you. Maybe it's a private journaling ritual or a meditation. Maybe it's sharing your joy with friends or family. Or perhaps it's treating yourself to something special when you reach a milestone. Whatever form it takes, the key is simple: keep acknowledging your progress. Every celebration reinforces the truth that you are growing, succeeding, and moving closer to your dream life.

The Power of Small Wins

Don't wait for major achievements to celebrate. The most successful people understand that progress is built on a foundation of small, consistent victories. Finished a difficult project? Celebrate. Had a productive conversation with a challenging colleague? Acknowledge it. Chose to exercise when you didn't feel like it? Recognize that demonstration of discipline.

These small celebrations create positive feedback loops, reinforcing successful behaviors and building confidence over time. They train your brain to notice and appreciate progress, making you more likely to continue growing and improving.

Progress, not perfection, is the strongest predictor of sustained effort and achievement. When you celebrate small wins, you create momentum that carries you through the inevitable challenges and setbacks of any meaningful pursuit.

Discovering Your Unique Awesomeness

Celebrating your wins isn't just a feel-good exercise, it has the power to transform many areas of your life. When you start acknowledging your accomplishments, big or small, you'll notice real changes. Be prepared: you may even discover your own awesomeness!

Each time you recognize an achievement, you reinforce a positive self-image and boost your confidence. You remind yourself of your strengths and abilities, naturally building a more empowering mindset. Often, you'll even uncover hidden gifts and talents you didn't realize you had.

Celebration is also a motivator. When you see your own progress, you feel inspired to set new goals and pursue them with greater energy. This momentum fuels higher productivity and renewed excitement in many areas of life.

Shifting your focus to wins also nurtures mental well-being. Instead of dwelling on what you haven't done, you anchor yourself in what you have achieved. This reduces stress and anxiety, cultivates a positive outlook, and gives you the strength to face future challenges. When obstacles arise, you'll have a history of success to lean on, proof that you're capable and resilient.

Celebrating wins can even strengthen your relationships. Sharing achievements with friends, family, or colleagues invites them into your joy and fosters a culture of encouragement and support. Success becomes a shared experience, deepening connection.

And don't underestimate the gratitude that comes from this practice. Acknowledging your progress naturally makes you more appreciative of your own efforts, the people who support you, and the opportunities that shape your journey. Gratitude then fuels even more growth and positivity.

Celebration doesn't need to be grand. A small ritual, a journal entry, or even a quiet moment of acknowledgment can create a powerful feedback loop of self-belief and momentum. Over time, this habit helps you meet challenges with optimism and resilience.

Remember: your awesomeness isn't about how skilled or talented you are, it's about your journey. Every challenge overcome, every skill learned, every failure turned into wisdom has shaped who you are today. Your struggles have built your strength, your persistence has created growth, and your experiences have given you wisdom. If that isn't worth celebrating, what is?

The Ripple Effect of Self-Confidence

When you silence your inner critic and embrace your awesomeness, the effects extend far beyond your personal experience. Confidence is contagious. When you believe in yourself, others are more likely to believe in you, too. When you celebrate your wins, you give others permission to celebrate theirs.

Your increased confidence enables you to take bigger risks, pursue more ambitious goals, and recover more quickly from setbacks. You become more creative, more collaborative, and more willing to step outside your comfort zone. You start saying yes to opportunities that previously would have terrified you.

The Choice Is Yours

You stand at a crossroads. One path is familiar, paved with self-doubt, limitation, and unfulfilled potential. Your inner critic knows it well and will gladly lead you down it. The other path is less certain but infinitely more exhilarating, the path of self-appreciation, growth, and limitless possibility.

This isn't a choice you make once. It's a choice you make daily. Each time you catch yourself in self-criticism, you can choose differently. Each time you accomplish something, you can choose to celebrate instead of dismiss it. Each time you face a challenge, you can choose to focus on your capabilities rather than your shortcomings.

Your inner critic may never disappear entirely. It has been part of you for too long. But you can learn to turn down its volume and amplify the voice of your inner champion. You can train yourself to see your successes, honor your growth, and embrace your unique awesomeness.

The question isn't whether you have the potential to achieve remarkable things, you do. The real question is: are you ready to stop believing the critic's lies? Are you ready to discover what you're truly capable of?

The journey begins with a single step: believing you are worthy of success, capable of growth, and deserving of compassion and celebration. Your future self, braver, freer, and more radiant than your critic could ever imagine, is waiting.

Remember: your power doesn't come from perfection. It comes from honoring every step you've already taken. Celebrate yourself, and you'll realize you've been awesome all along.

Start today. Open your Celebration Journal and write down at least three wins. Then, if you'd like, share them with me on my socials or by email. I'd love to celebrate with you!

ABOUT THE AUTHOR

PIA BECKER

Pia Becker, known as the Dream Manifestation Mentor, is the founder of *Dream and Wanderland*. Her chapter, "Embrace Your Awesomeness Through Celebrating Wins," in *The Power Within* offers a fresh approach to empowering women, helping them reignite their inner passion, break through limitations, and bring their most extraordinary dreams to life. Celebrating wins is more than focusing on achievements—it's a way to remember how incredible you are, what you're capable of, and that anything is possible.

With her grounded, hands-on approach, Pia breaks even the boldest visions into tangible, actionable steps, making big dreams feel achievable rather than overwhelming. This is the very system she has used time and again for herself, whether planning to travel the world or making her own dreams a reality. Her mission is to inspire a life of freedom, purpose, and soulful adventure.

Connect with Pia:
Visit my website: dreamandwanderland.com
Follow my adventures: instagram.com/dreamandwanderland
Share your wins via email: dreamandwanderland@gmail.com

13

AWAKENING THE SELF
FINDING POWER IN THE JOURNEY

BY SUELYNN SILVA

"Dreams aren't built by chance—they're shaped by belief, action, and the courage to shine your light."

Awakening to Myself

My transformation began when I was with my current husband and our third child was about two years old. I had worked many jobs before, but at this point, we decided I would stay home with my son. Somewhere in that season, I disappeared—not just from the world, but from myself.

My days were swallowed by constant sobbing, chores, and television. I loved my children passionately and would do anything for them to feel that love. I loved my family. But I had lost my sense of purpose. Life felt flat, like I was moving through a fog—waiting for something, anything, to shift.

Then, one ordinary day, a sudden wave of clarity washed over me. Out of nowhere, I blurted to my husband:

"This is not my life. This is not what I'm meant to be doing. My life should be different. My life is more than this."

The words felt like a spark—small, yet fierce—and they ignited something inside me I hadn't felt in years.

Only a few days later, a letter arrived that would change everything. The words on the page hit me like lightning:

"You are not living the life you were meant to live."

It included five short stories and an invitation to buy a book I couldn't afford. Yet deep inside, I knew: this book would change everything.

I showed the letter to my dad. He read it carefully, said nothing, and walked out. When he returned, he handed me the money and said only this:

"This works. Take it."

I discovered that my dad had just won the money at the casino. It felt like the universe itself was conspiring to wake me up.

When the book finally arrived, I almost dropped it. It was a thousand pages thick. I had never finished a book that big. But the moment I started reading, something inside me stirred.

The words leapt off the page, speaking directly to me:

You are special.

You can make a difference.

You can lead yourself.

It was all about self-leadership, a revolutionary idea. For the first time, I realized I didn't have to stay stuck. I could think for myself, make my own choices, and create the life I wanted.

Over the next nine months, two more books arrived. I read each one twice, first by myself, then again with my husband. With every page, something inside me began to shift. The tears that had weighed me down slowly stopped. My energy, like fire in my bones, returned. My curiosity stirred awake, like a long-dormant spark finally catching flame.

I couldn't get enough of learning. Quantum physics, consciousness, philosophy, health, longevity, I devoured it all. Life itself became a playground, full of discovery. And through it all, one profound truth revealed itself, a truth that has guided me ever since: **growth is not a destination—it is the journey itself.**

Creating a New Reality

A few years later, after moving from Las Vegas to Washington to start a new life, my journey took another leap forward. My husband and I were diving deep into creating our reality, truly understanding how the Law of Attraction works.

The CDs we listened to challenged us, saying things like, *set a goal, make a vision board, and focus on it with excitement.* At the time, it felt impossible. The odds seemed stacked against us. But still, we put our vision on the board: the house of our dreams. The full acre we wanted, a fenced yard, a four-car garage, and a big office. At first, it felt outrageous even to imagine it, but we did more than imagine. We believed. We aligned. We worked. We held the picture in our hearts with excitement and anticipation.

And then, it happened. Against all odds, we bought the house we had dreamed of. Every detail matched our vision: the acre, the fence, the garage, the office. Walking through it for the first time, I ran my hands along the cool wooden banisters, heard my kids laughing in the open yard, and breathed in the earthy scent of the land that was now ours.

It wasn't just a house. It was living, breathing proof that our thoughts—and our belief in them—can shape our reality.

At the same time, something else was stirring inside me. My passion for health was growing stronger with each passing day. I had wrestled with digestive issues for as long as I could remember, always searching for answers, always trying to feel better, always chasing that elusive sense of well-being.

That search led me deeper, beyond symptoms, into the delicate balance between mind, body, and energy. I began to see that this journey wasn't just about my own health. It was bigger than me. It was a calling.

I wanted to help others feel whole, to guide them toward transformation, just as I was learning to guide myself. That's when I took the first step on my health coaching journey, enrolling in classes to become both a coach and an energy healer, ready to turn my struggles into purpose.

Dreambuilding the Next Chapter

After my youngest son graduated from high school, my husband and I found ourselves at a crossroads, wondering what the next chapter of our lives would look like. We both felt an undeniable pull to return to Las Vegas, to be closer to my brother, sister-in-law, niece, and nephew. Family had always been my anchor, and the thought of reconnecting more deeply with them filled me with a quiet, joyful excitement.

We had done this before—set a vision, built a dream board, and watched life open doors in ways we never could have imagined. When we bought our house in Washington, it seemed impossible at first, but our vision held us steady, guiding us through. Now, once again, we pulled out the poster board, the glitter, the magazines, and the markers. It was time to create a new picture of what we wanted.

This time, though, it wasn't just about a house. It was about freedom. We wanted more than a home, we wanted comfort, freedom, a life of flexibility and adventure. The picture was clear: sell our house and buy an RV, one that offered enough space and comfort to truly live in, but also gave us the freedom to roam, and to explore.

We began attending RV shows, browsing online, snapping photos, touching the countertops, and walking through the layouts—dreambuilding. For me, dreambuilding isn't just about shopping; it's about training your mind and heart to believe that something is already yours.

Then came the synchronicity that still makes me smile. We put our house on the market, expecting a long process. Maybe a few months, we thought. But it sold in just seventeen hours. Just like that, we had twenty-one days to move.

The very next day after accepting the offer, we headed to another RV show. As we walked through the aisles, something caught our eye—an RV with a porch, an outdoor sink, and even an outdoor kitchen. We stopped dead in our tracks. When we pulled up the photos on our phones, we realized it was the exact same RV we had taken pictures of and fallen in love with just few months earlier.

In that moment, I felt a chill run through my spine. My heart raced, my breath caught, and I couldn't stop smiling. I was so amazed. It felt as if the universe had winked at us, saying, Y*ou dreamed it. You believed it. And now it's yours.*

We bought it. And just like that, life moved us back to Las Vegas three months earlier than we had planned. The timing felt divine. Looking back, I believe the universe knew something we didn't— that every moment with Levi and our family mattered, and those extra months turned out to be a gift beyond measure.

When Grief Finds You

We had five beautiful months in Las Vegas before my world shattered. Those months were full of family dinners, laughter, and everyday moments that now feel like precious treasures. I thought we had all the time in the world—time for camping trips, celebrations, and endless adventures together.

Then, my brother Levi's life was tragically cut short, and everything changed. He was twelve years younger than me, but as we grew older, our bond deepened. He became my partner in philosophy, my confidant, my co-explorer in conversations about consciousness, manifestation, and what it truly means to live fully. Levi had a way of filling life with love, adventure, and a kind of presence that made everything seem brighter.

Levi was a theater major who helped found a theater company in Las Vegas more than twenty years ago. When we gathered to celebrate his life at the UNLV theater, over four hundred people filled the space. The room was alive with stories—funny, heartfelt, unforgettable. In true Levi fashion, someone even dressed up as Bigfoot, a playful nod to his recent fascination with the elusive creature. Guests wore buttons featuring Sasquatch, a heart, and the words **#LiveLikeLevi**—a joyful reminder of the love, kindness, and fun he spread wherever he went. To this day, we leave those buttons in places we visit, a piece of him we carry with us.

His passing blindsided me. For months, I felt like that lost version of myself again—the one buried in grief and suffocating invisibility. But this time was different. I had tools. I had a path. And I knew Levi would want me to keep moving forward, to carry his joy into the world instead of letting grief swallow me whole.

From Chaos to Clarity

Through it all, I carry deep gratitude for my family, for the lessons, and for the path itself. My three grown children and my grandchild may still live in Washington, but distance has never weakened our bond. We speak often, and their love reminds me every day that connection stretches far beyond miles.

I am just as grateful for my husband, who walks this journey by my side. His steady encouragement has been a light in the moments when the work felt overwhelming. And now, as my bond with my sister-in-law, niece, and nephew grows stronger, I see how priceless family truly is.

But make no mistake, this work is not for the faint of heart. Moving from chaos to clarity demands facing darkness head-on and walking straight through it. Personal growth asks you to strip away the layers, confront the shadows, and discover what you're truly made of. In that process, I uncovered something I never knew I carried: a resilience and courage that had been waiting for me all along.

One of the greatest turning points came when I chose to take full responsibility for my life. No more blame. No more guilt. Just ownership. That decision was radical, but it set me free.

For too long, I had seen myself through the lens of limitation. I told myself I wasn't good enough, not smart enough, too quiet, too invisible. But on this path, I began to see myself differently, as someone bigger. I began to affirm: I am not small. I am not powerless. I am an infinite being, capable of creating, growing, and becoming more than I ever imagined.

That shift required something deeper—radical self-honesty. It was not easy to face the ways I had hidden, the times I had settled, or the voices I had believed and allowed to shape me. But harder than all of that was learning how to stop beating myself up.

The truth is, most of the time we say things to ourselves; negative, cruel things that we would never say to a friend. I was no different. I was an expert in this. But my turning point came the day I stood in front of a mirror, looked myself in the eyes, and whispered words I had never dared to believe before: *"I love you."*

It may sound small, but for me, that was all I need to alter my life. My throat tightened, my chest ached, and tears spilled down my cheeks as those words fell out my mouth. Something inside me cracked open, something that had been shut away for decades.

As a child, I was painfully shy. I molded myself to fit into everyone else's description of me, never my own. I was afraid of drawing too much attention. But somewhere along the way, I carried a secret desire that terrified me: I wanted to be a speaker.

At the time, the thought felt impossible, almost laughable. Yet I've learned that when you set an intention, the universe responds. Slowly, opportunities began to appear in unexpected ways. I found myself mentoring others, sharing my voice, my lessons, and my encouragement, first in quiet spaces, then in places that kept growing larger.

I was leading calls, speaking on webinars, and sharing my story in the same Mastermind community that had once given me the books that started this transformation years ago. Each step built my confidence, each moment pushing me past the limits I once believed I had.

Then came the clients, the people who trusted me with their own transformations. One man joined me for a 21-day detox. He had been on heartburn medication for years, and it no longer worked. After the program, he not only felt lighter and more energized, but he was able to stop the medication altogether.

Another client confided that she had been trapped in a relationship that wasn't healthy for her. Through our work together, she found the strength to walk away, and later met someone who was truly aligned with her heart.

Others lost weight, gained energy, or simply learned how to treat themselves with more kindness. The physical changes are wonderful, of course, but what moves me most is witnessing their spirits come alive again—seeing them reclaim their joy and remember who they really are, piece by piece.

And slowly, I began to realize something life-changing: I didn't have to hide anymore. I could step into the light without hesitation. I could connect deeply with others. I could share my gifts with the world. And the more I did, the stronger the transformation became, not just for me this time, but for the people walking this path with me.

Integrating What I Have Learned into a Holistic Method

The most exciting part of this journey has been the learning itself. How beautiful it was to learn the things I learned back then. After reading those three thousand pages all those years ago, something inside me opened in a way that never closed again. It was a deep, unshakable love for learning, discovering, and exploring new possibilities.

Because of my lifelong gut issues, I became my first client. I was searching for answers, trying detoxes and herbal protocols, experimenting with ways to feel better. That curiosity pushed me to study the gut more deeply.

Science has shown in recent years how powerful the connection between the gut and the brain really is. When I began testing my own gut health, I was shocked to see how strongly an imbalanced gut could be linked to conditions like ADHD, depression, and anxiety.

This knowledge lit a fire inside me. I realized healing isn't just physical—it's mental, emotional, and energetic. Alongside diet changes, toxin removal, and following protocols, I began exploring higher consciousness practices and nervous system regulation.

And that's when I noticed something profound: addressing both the body and the mind at the same time created incredible results.

That realization became the foundation for the method I now share with others. It's a holistic approach that doesn't focus on just one piece of the puzzle but sees the whole picture—body, mind, and energy working together.

Out of this, I built my signature program:

- **Rebalance** the body through nutrition, detoxing, and natural healing.
- **Rewire** subconscious beliefs that keep you stuck in old patterns.
- **Reclaim** life with renewed clarity, energy, and purpose.

This work lights me up because I know what it feels like to struggle. I know what it feels like to be unseen while present, to carry pain quietly, and to search for answers that don't seem to come. I also know the beauty of coming alive again, of moving from chaos into clarity, and of finding your power where you once felt powerless. Guiding others on that journey is not just what I do, it is who I am. It is my calling.

Your journey is waiting.

Change is possible at any stage of life, no matter what you've been through, if you are willing to step into your own strength. You don't have to wait for the perfect moment or for clarity to magically arrive. It begins with a single choice—the decision to believe you are capable, worthy, and ready to create something new.

Take a moment today. Stand in front of the mirror, look deeply and ask yourself: What life do I truly want to live? Then take one small step in that direction. Follow it with another. Each decision carries you forward. Each moment becomes a chance to awaken your courage, your strength, and your joy.

Your path is already here. All that's left is to step into it and embrace what's waiting for you.

ABOUT THE AUTHOR
SUELYNN SILVA

Suelynn Silva is a High-Performance Mind-Body Coach who helps people rebalance their health, rewire their mindset, and reclaim vibrant, purposeful lives. She combines science, functional medicine, and practical energy work to create real, lasting transformation.

Her own journey showed her that true healing goes far beyond diet or exercise—it's about addressing the body, mind, and energy as a whole. Through this process, she learned how to let go of old patterns, restore balance, and step fully into the person she was meant to become. That awakening became her life's calling.

Today, Suelynn guides others through one-on-one functional coaching and her signature program, Rebalance • Rewire • Reclaim. She blends functional medicine, health and longevity coaching, life coaching, and energy practices—including Dr. Sue Morter's Energy Codes®, breathwork, and EFT—to tailor meaningful, real and lasting change for each individual.

As a teacher, mentor, writer, and speaker, she leads workshops, Zoom classes, and collaborative group courses, while also co-creating content for YouTube and podcasts. Her mission is to help people move beyond stress, fatigue, and overwhelm, stepping confidently into alignment, vitality, and a life that feels fully alive and extraordinary in every way.

Connect with Suelynn:
Website: integratedhealthysolutions.com
Email: integratedhealthysolutions@gmail.com

14

WE HAVE A VOICE, AND WE CAN USE IT.

TERRI TONKIN

Using your voice is a powerful tool. It allows you to stand up for what you believe in and inspire others to do the same.

*– **Michelle Obama***

For far too long, women have been ignored and silenced. Over time, culture and society have taught many women they don't have a voice, that their opinions aren't worth hearing. In many places and periods, women who spoke out were sometimes punished brutally. Yet others, those who kept speaking despite the danger, were eventually heard.

When a woman speaks, she speaks with conviction and with passion. She believes in what she says.

Remember the Suffragettes? For those who may be too young to remember, they were a group of women who were activists in the late 1800s and early 1900s who campaigned and fought for the right to vote. Many were jailed for their beliefs, and for speaking up; some suffered terribly, and some died. Still, they persisted. Their courage sparked a movement that changed laws and shifted minds. In a man's world, they demanded to be seen and heard, and in time, they were.

That is the power of women who come together to change our society. No woman should ever believe her voice is unworthy. It takes one voice to start the process of change.

Don't let the noise of others' opinions drown out your own inner voice. – **Steve Jobs**

Think back through your life and remember a time when you felt unworthy of being heard.

As a teenager in high school, I wasn't really a girly girl. I loved working in the yard and tending to the vegetable garden with my dad. I loved the hum of the engine when he worked on the car or small engines, the smell of oil and soil, and the steady way his hands moved. I was always right there beside him. At home, I learned to cook from both my parents; my mum taught me how to wash my clothes, iron them, and do simple sewing, while my dad taught me practical skills I still use today. I am grateful for those lessons.

At school, when it came time to choose subjects, I asked for woodwork and metalwork because I loved them passionately. The answer was blunt: that would never happen. I was relegated to home economics, which meant sewing and cooking, because well, they said I was a girl. Girls don't take trades. It felt like the door had been slammed shut on me.

It took about thirty-five years for that to change. Girls today have a wide range of subjects to choose from, including trades. Maybe I was a catalyst for that change. I like to think so.

When I had to think about my future, I felt unsure of which path to follow. I had always wanted to be a teacher, and I earned enough points in my final year, through grades and assessments, to pursue that dream. I was accepted into a three-year Special Education course to train as a teacher for children with special needs. I was particularly drawn to working with the deaf community at that time. Yet, even as I accepted that place, I wasn't sure I still wanted that dream.

I had sat for, and passed, the entrance exams for the public service and two banks. I had been offered a full-time position with a film laboratory, a role I'd been working in since finishing school, helping to set up a new laboratory in a new location. I had also applied for, and passed, the entrance and medical requirements to join the defence forces.

I had options available to me. Some were the conventional "girl jobs," and some weren't. Back then, in the mid-1970s, society expected girls to choose traditional female roles like clerical work, teaching, or nursing. But once again, I went against the norm. I made a choice that felt right for me: I enlisted in the defence forces.

Recruit training lasted just over five weeks. Then it was on to 'trade' training, where I ended up learning how to type, something I had never touched in high school. Typing, I was amazed, wasn't even something I had considered. I hadn't taken any commercial subjects. Oh, I was a rebel. Instead, I focused on academic subjects that would keep my options open, ensuring I wouldn't be pushed into one of those "girl jobs" that society had in mind for me.

I loved being part of that world, and if circumstances were different, I would've gladly served longer than I did. However, back then, women weren't encouraged to remain in the service. If you got married, especially to another serving member, you became an extra appendage for the man, or worse still, a handbag. My husband was determined to make the defence force his career, and I had to jump through hoops just to marry him. The idea of having children, with maternity leave still in its early stages, felt like another hoop I wasn't prepared to leap through. Besides, the chance of us ever being posted together to the same unit seemed impossible.

So, we made the decision that I would leave and forgo my defence career for his. It wasn't a choice we made lightly, but the world was different back then. Soon after, he was posted to a new unit, and I stepped into the role of a defence spouse.

I remember attending a meeting for the wives of servicemen, and oh my goodness, the complaints, what a chorus of whining women they were. I wasn't sure whether to laugh or cringe. As an ex-serving member, I couldn't resist stirring the pot. I'd put on my devil's advocate hat and brought up the issues no one seemed willing to talk about, the ones everyone else preferred to ignore or gloss over.

Some of the women would complain about their husbands being moved to a new unit every two or three years. Well, hello, you married a serviceman. These men were relocated where they were needed, when they were needed. Some women struggled with the constant moves, especially when it meant their children had to change schools so often. I get it; it could be difficult, I'm sure. But there was a beautiful side to it, too. We had the chance to experience new locations, meet new people, explore different cultures, and take part in unique activities. It was such a wonderful way to receive an education schools couldn't offer. Instead of focusing on the hardships, we needed to learn how to embrace the adventure. We had to start seeing the benefits of these relocations.

For some, leaving extended family behind was the hardest part. But for us, the beauty of relocating time and time again brought us something special. We met with new families at each new place. These weren't just neighbours, but people who became lifelong friends. After nearly fifty years, we're still connected with so many of them. Moving also gave us a chance to declutter, to leave behind the things we no longer needed.

Never be afraid to raise your voice for honesty and truth and compassion against injustice and lying and greed. If people all over the world would do this, it would change the earth. **—William Faulkner**

Over the years, frequent relocating required me to take on various jobs in different locations. I worked in retail, supermarkets, hardware stores, and truck and tractor spares. But for the longest time, I found my home in the banking industry. Despite the challenges of moving four times across three states, I was fortunate to stay with the bank for 14 years.

After leaving the finance world, I transitioned into a government-funded youth program, where I helped young school leavers navigate their paths to further education, training, or employment. This was the work I was most passionate about. I truly loved it because it felt like I was making a real difference in their lives, guiding them toward a brighter, more sustainable future. While the work itself was demanding, the sense of fulfillment was indescribable.

In this role, I used my voice every day. I advocated for these young people within the school system and fought for them when it came to securing employment opportunities. I also found myself needing to convince their parents, helping them understand why supporting their children's dreams was so crucial.

I was working with a young man who had some learning difficulties, but he was a truly lovely person. He had a strong desire to be independent and earn his place in the community, yet his parents were understandably worried about how he would manage once he left school, especially when it came to fitting into the workplace.

To help him, I reached out to a local employer who worked for a national company. I explained the situation with this young man; he was a literal learner. He could handle one task at a time, but when multiple tasks were presented to him, it overwhelmed him, leaving him confused about which task to focus on. After our conversation, we agreed that a work experience placement would be a great opportunity. It would allow the employer to see firsthand how he worked and figure out the best way to support him moving forward.

The young man spent a week on work experience at the company, and then we arranged for him to attend once a week for ongoing exposure and to keep the momentum going. The employer made sure he was well taken care of, offering him different tasks, but always one at a time. Over time, it became clear that this young man was a good fit for the workplace, and he was happy in the environment.

The employer was so impressed that they asked me to help arrange a school-based traineeship in warehousing for him. By the time he finished school, the traineeship had transitioned into a full-time position with ongoing training. A true win-win-win for everyone.

Another young man was referred to me for help. He was struggling and failing at school. He'd barely passed Year 9, failed Year 10, and things weren't looking much better for Year 11. I could see the weight of it on him, the pressure of expectations and the fear of falling further behind. So, I sat down with this young man, hoping to understand what he truly wanted to do.

I reached out to the school, trying to find a solution that would allow him to stay connected to his education while gaining some real-world work experience. It was clear he needed something different, something more practical to keep him engaged. The system wasn't working for him as it stood.

Then, I had a conversation with his parents. They were set on the idea that he needed to stay in school to finish Year 12. It wasn't easy to challenge their beliefs, especially when they only saw the traditional route as the answer. But I explained gently that if things didn't change, if he continued down this same path, he would walk away with little more than an attendance certificate.

I worked closely with an employer, the school, and his parents to arrange work experience for him, three days a week at the job and two at school. He worked hard and earned the respect of his employer. This arrangement lasted for several months until the employer asked if he could start paying the young man and have him work on Saturdays as well. We set up a school-based traineeship to make that possible.

The young man truly blossomed during this time. Eventually, he left school when his traineeship transitioned into a full-time role. He didn't finish Year 11, let alone Year 12. Yet, against the odds, he went on to complete an apprenticeship in welding and fabrication.

Years later, his mother reached out to express her gratitude. That young man, once struggling to find his way, went on to work for one of the biggest boat builders in Australia, and he's never looked back.

This experience had a lasting impact on me, and advocating for young people has become one of my deepest passions.

I should also mention how my dad shaped the way I approach life. He always encouraged me to think for myself, never just agreeing because someone else said I should. One of the ways he did this was by teaching my brothers and I to form an opinion but also to understand why we held it. If we came to him with a problem, he wouldn't just offer a solution. Instead, he'd ask, "What do you think the solution is?" He believed that we could all have an opinion, but we needed to back it up with thoughtful reasoning. Then, he'd debate it with us, ensuring we fully under-stood what we believed. It was a challenging but rewarding way to learn.

Have you ever heard the saying, "If you never ask, the answer is always no"?

When I worked in public service, my husband was employed by Virgin Airlines. He was based in Brisbane, Queensland, while his boss was located in Perth, Western Australia (the other side of the country). Occasionally, he was required to work out of the Perth airport, which meant he would be away for weeks or even months at a time.

I vividly remember one particular occasion when he was scheduled to be in Perth for two months. It was a difficult time, and I mustered up the courage to ask my department head if there was any possibility I could work from the Perth office for six weeks to be with him.

My manager asked if I knew anyone at the Perth office. Fortunately, I did. I called my contact there, explained my situation, and inquired if there was any way to make it work. They were understanding and assured me they had plenty of available desks and could easily accommodate me.

With their confirmation, my manager reached out to the Perth office manager, and it was agreed that I could travel and continue my work, just in a different location for six weeks.

I asked my contact about the dress code, knowing that each branch had its own minimum standards. Given the varying climates across locations, those standards could differ. In Queensland, where the summer heat and humidity were relentless, my summer work attire consisted of business shorts, a business shirt, and appropriate footwear. Perth, on the other hand, could be cool and windy or hot and dry.

So, I inquired if dressing similarly in Perth due to the varying climate would be acceptable.

To my surprise, I was told that no woman had ever worn shorts to work. I pressed further, asking if it would be alright to wear them. The response was cautiously approving: "Yes, you can, but the manager will let you know if it's not appropriate."

Well, let me tell you, the manager had no issue with it. The women in the office? They thought it was a brilliant idea, even though, to my knowledge, no one had ever dared to try it before. I had become a rule-breaker.

When I walked through the business district of Perth, I couldn't help but notice that no women were wearing shorts. It simply wasn't a thing at the time. Maybe things have changed now.

Looking back, I wonder if I was a disruptor. Or, perhaps, as they'd call it today, an influencer (though that term didn't even exist back then).

We all have a voice. Some a whisper, some a roar. If you can roar, roar for others. If you can only whisper, keep trying. Every roar started small. – **M.L. Shanahan**

As I mentioned earlier, women have been conditioned not to speak up or speak out. Many of us were shaped to be 'people pleasers'— that is, to keep the peace, avoid causing any upset, and make sure everyone else's needs were met and that they were happy, even at the cost of our own. We were taught to know our place, to avoid stepping out of line. We couldn't have our own opinions, and if we did, we were expected to keep them to ourselves, especially if they contradicted a man's. A woman's role was clear: to take care of the man, the family, and the home.

One of my favorite things to say about finding our voice is this: "NO" is a complete sentence. We all need to establish personal and professional boundaries to protect ourselves from those people-pleasing situations. As women, it's vital that we embrace this. We don't have to say yes to everything, all the time. And we certainly don't owe anyone an explanation when we say NO.

I have a right to say "no" to anything if I am not ready, if it feels unsafe, or if it violates my boundaries and my values. In other words, I have a right to boundaries. – **Jef Gazley**

Here are some helpful ways to say no.

- I really wish I could help; however, I am not available at that time.
- What a great idea. It's a shame I'll have to decline the invitation.
- Thank you for asking me, but I have other plans.
- I am grateful you considered me for the project, but I am committed with other ventures.
- I'm not in a position to say yes right now.
- Thank you for the opportunity however I will have to pass.
- I have no capacity to take on new work at the moment.
- Not this time, but keep me in mind for any future events.

When we say no, we don't owe anyone an explanation. It's okay to simply say NO. Remember: "NO." is a complete sentence.

Never be afraid to use your voice to make a difference. Your story, unlike any other, has the power to change the world. – ***Amanda Bernardo***

It's not always easy or comfortable to use our voice. The fear of speaking in public, or even speaking up, is one of the most common fears we face. We fear being judged. We fear criticism. We fear being unheard or ridiculed. Trust me, I understand; I've been there.

While I loved sharing my knowledge, skills or experiences, whether training staff or leading workshops, I feared stepping onto the stage to deliver my message. I'd break out in a hot sweat, my hands would shake, my stomach would twist from being nervous, and I'd feel like I might faint. It felt like everything was crashing down at that moment. These reactions, though, are normal. They're natural for everyone, even the seasoned speakers who've done this a thousand times. And let's be honest: they probably still feel a bit of it, even if it's just to a lesser extent.

To conquer this fear, I decided to take action. I enrolled in speaker training, committing to a three-day immersive course. The challenge? I had to prepare a ten-minute presentation. I would present it to a group of about 30 people, receive their feedback, present it again, get feedback from the trainer, and then present it once more, this time in front of a larger audience. And on top of all that? I'd be filmed. OMG!

Talk about nerves. I was sweating bricks, wondering how I was ever going to get through it. Yet, somehow, I did. The audience was incredible, offering valuable feedback on how my words sounded and felt to them. The trainers also provided insightful feedback on my technique, positioning, tone, content, and context.

By the end of those three days, I was hooked. Yes, I still had butterflies in my stomach, but instead of letting that nervous energy overwhelm me, I channeled it into excitement. What a buzz!

Not long after the training, I had the chance to give an on-stage presentation at IGNITE, Brisbane. It was similar to a mini-TEDx. I had ten minutes, five slides (visuals only, no words), and a microphone. The nerves hit again, but once more, it was an incredible experience.

These days, if I'm asked to speak, I almost never say no. Since that first training and stage experience, I've been interviewed countless times on Zoom calls, Facebook Lives, and podcasts, both in Australia and the USA. I've presented workshops and led information sessions at meet-ups and networking events. And what I've learned through it all is this: what I have to say and share truly matters to others.

However, my favourite way to use my voice remains through my writing.

I write in the non-fiction genres of lifestyle, well-being, personal and professional development, and memoir. At the age of 60, I finally fulfilled a life-long dream: to write my own book.

I have always been an avid reader, from a very young age. Growing up in the remote outback of western Queensland, my family had a radio to listen to but no television. Reading became my escape. My parents, understanding the value of books, encouraged my passion by regularly buying me new ones. That early love of reading has stayed with me throughout my life, and now, I often have two books on the go, one non-fiction and one fiction, or sometimes two non-fiction books.

Recently, I worked as a judge for The ABLE Golden Book Awards here in Australia, which has expanded my reading list far beyond what I would typically choose. In just over six weeks, I've read 50 books, ranging from children's literature to memoirs, mysteries, and educational texts. The experience has been both interesting and satisfying, as well as eye-opening, broadening my understanding of genres and storytelling.

Returning to my own writing journey, I've always known I wanted to write my own book, and I was fortunate to achieve that dream some years ago. Since then, I've contributed a chapter to more than 20 compilation books, all within the non-fiction realm. Some of these books originated in Australia, while others have come from overseas, including the USA and Singapore.

I've written chapters on perspectives, gratitude, forgiveness, influence, success, authenticity, enlightenment, the impact of suicide, soul mates, mindset, inspiration, identity, and ghostwriting.

One of my proudest achievements was assisting in the development and writing of a book for our local Returned Services League (RSL) branch. It focused on the military history of the region, and as a veteran, it felt like a way to give back to the community. The goal was to create a resource that would help younger generations learn about our history while also raising funds to support veterans and current service members. What began as a project where I thought I'd simply be doing the writing turned into something much more. It involved extensive research and connecting with the community to share the rich history of the region.

As I've mentioned before, I've had the privilege of being interviewed on podcasts, where I shared my wisdom and experiences. I've also been published in magazines, using my voice to distill complex information and share the lessons I've learned.

I'm the author of two non-fiction books. The first is a memoir titled *My Time to Shine: Your Voice, Your Choice, Your Life,* and the second is about well-being, called *HAPPINESS: Your Choice to Choose, 100+ Ways.*

My Time to Shine tells my story from childhood to age 60 *(maybe I should've called it Zero to Sixty).* In it, I reflect on the various roles and responsibilities I've taken on throughout my life, roles that were either chosen by me or imposed upon me. The underlying theme of this book is that these roles have shaped who I am today, but they don't define me. I am so much more than that.

My second book, *HAPPINESS,* was over 30 years in the making. The turning point came when I lost my brother to suicide. It was during this time that I felt compelled to dive deeper into personal development and human behavior. I realized there had to be a way to help others, ways to free them from the isolation of unhappiness.

In this book, I've compiled over 100 strategies to help people move away from unhappiness, drawn from my own self-awareness, research, and countless discussions with peers and clients. My hope is that it serves as a helpful guide for anyone who picks it up, whether they're struggling themselves or simply seeking a path toward a better mindset.

This is a book that doesn't need to be read from cover to cover. You can start at any chapter that speaks to you, or open to any page where you believe your solution lies. There, you'll find a strategy ready for you to try. It's meant to be a resource you can return to whenever you need it. I trust that through these words, many will find hope and healing. After all, saving even one person from the pain of suicide is a gift, something for which I am forever grateful.

I understand that finding your voice may not be easy, especially if you've been silenced for so long. I want to remind you that the journey starts with small steps. Take a few, then a few more. Keep moving forward, and soon, your speaking muscle will grow stronger.

As Maxwell Smart from the '70s show *Get Smart* used to say, "Use your power for good, not evil." Use your voice in truth, and use it in positive ways to make a meaningful impact.

Remember: You have a voice. You can use it. It is worthy of being heard.

ABOUT THE AUTHOR
TERRI TONKIN

Terri Tonkin is a multiple international best-selling author, ghostwriter, and life coach dedicated to empowering others through the written word and personal growth. Specializing in non-fiction, she has authored her own books, contributed to numerous collaborative projects, and developed manuscripts that bring other people's stories to life.

Featured in various magazines and interviewed on multiple podcasts, Terri shares insights that inspire and motivate audiences worldwide. As the founder and face of Connect Within, she has created a safe and supportive space where clients feel heard, validated, and encouraged to discover the solutions they seek. Her mission is to inspire others to embrace their potential and live with purpose.

A lifelong learner with a passion for reading and travel, Terri draws on her own journey of triumphs and challenges to guide and uplift those she serves.

Connect with Terri:
Facebook: facebook.com/terri.tonkin.3
LinkedIn: linkedin.com/in/terri-tonkin
Email: terri@connectwithin.com

Be Part of Something Extraordinary

The **Women's Empower Network** (**WEN**) is more than a group — it's a global movement of women standing together in Support, Mentorship, Leadership, and Empowerment.

Inside our private community, members share wisdom through live interviews, events, roundtables, and more.

We lift one another through mentorship, collaboration, and celebration.

If you're ready to grow, connect, and rise with women who are leading from the heart — you belong here.

The Power Series Invitation
A Journey of Strength, Vision, and Legacy

The Power Series is a collection of annual multi-author books created through WEN.

Each volume brings together courageous voices from around the world — stories of resilience, transformation, and leadership.

These books are more than stories — they are guideposts for women rising into their own power.

*Scan the QR Code
to visit WomensEmpower.Network.com*

Together, we rise — one story, one voice, one vision at a time.

www.ingramcontent.com/pod-product-compliance
Lightning Source LLC
Chambersburg PA
CBHW051513120626
46551CB00012B/902